Praise for *Be Seen Now!*

This useful and well-written book helped me find what is unique about my speaking content and style. It helped me connect my heart to my theories and communicate why the things I speak about are important to me.
—Susan Campbell, PhD, author of *Getting Real* and *From Triggered to Tranquil*

In a world where change is rampant and fear can set in, Lee draws a connection between you and the audience that is charismatic. Public speaking becomes a spiritual experience, where you co-create with your listeners.
—Helene Lerner, founder of WomenWorking.com, author of *Time for Me: Self-Care and Simple Pleasures for Women Who Do Too Much*

I recommend this book to all leaders and to anyone who wants to speak authentically in groups, meetings, and presentations.
—Sandra Zimmer, author of *It's Your Time to Shine: How to Overcome Fear of Public Speaking, Develop Authentic Presence and Speak from Your Heart*

Ayurvedic medicine says that speaking who you are improves your health. Expressing yourself fully increases your Agni (digestion), improves heart circulation and moods. Suppression of your voice represses your innate power. *Be Seen Now!* charts a practical path to living your healthiest self out loud.
—Cynthia Copple, author of *Know Your Blueprint: The Ayurvedic Secret to Restoring Your Vitality and Passion*

I highly recommend *Be Seen Now!* to anyone who wants to feel more present, relaxed, and self-assured as a speaker.
—John Amodeo, author of *Dancing with Fire: A Mindful Way to Loving Relationships*

I no longer endure a pre-performance anxiety headache, nor do I find myself overthinking public appearance ahead of time. *Be Seen Now!* adeptly guides the reader in the direction of authentic leadership.
—Nina Krebs, author of *Shades of Love and Loss: Caring for a Partner with Dementia*

Lee Glickstein makes a strong case for starting speeches with a personal story to build instant rapport. As the saying goes, people don't care what you know until they know you care. *Be Seen Now!* offers many great ways for speakers to show their audiences they care.

—Dan Janal, author of *Write Your Book in a Flash!*

This is a beautiful book that honors the true value of human beings and invites us to express ourselves from the place of innate magnificence that is inside each of us. Lee has a magnificent life calling in assisting people to open up their natural abilities to communicate. Highly recommended.

—Marilyn Gordon, author of *Realize Your Greatness: A Spectacular Journey to Success, Transformation, and Spiritual Power*

This book is the perfect prescription for speakers who want to improve their delivery and presence with audiences. I love the "lack of technique" approach—it's easy, natural, and uplifting. It will influence my speaking going forward.

—Robert G. Kramer, author of *Taming the Black Dog of Depression: A Guide for Those Who Are Suffering and Their Families*

I cannot recommend this new book more highly—it is truly a gem, filled with incredible wisdom that invites readers to take their communication skills to a much deeper and higher level, which will offer profound rewards for all who take his gentle, thoughtful ideas and wonderful insights to heart and put them into daily practice."

—Caroline Joy Adams, author of *The Power to Write: Seven Keys to Discover Your Writer Within*

Breathing, eye availability, and being fully present in the room are just the beginning of the gold Lee offers. These practices will not only make you a better speaker but also a better listener in everyday life.

—Michelle Vandepas, author of *Purpose: The Alignment Guide*

I'm getting a copy of this breakthrough book for every young speaker I know, and some of the old ones. It clarifies what I've known as a professional speaker for thirty years, that when we can drop into a deeper level of ourselves, we have a good time and people get who we are. When I present from this place I feel like my words and presence are touching people.
—Dale Ledbetter, author of *From Mother with Love* and
How Wall Street Rips You Off—and What You Can Do to Defend Yourself

Be Seen Now! is a must-read for anyone seeking to elevate their communication and leadership skills by breaking free from public speaking anxiety and truly connecting with their audiences. Glickstein doesn't just teach you how to speak; he shows you how to be seen and heard for who you truly are.
—Kathleen Gage, author of *Power Up for Profits*

What I love about Lee Glickstein's work is that he goes way beyond the tips and techniques of public speaking. Being an effective speaker has so little to do with technique and everything to do with the consciousness we are speaking from. *Be Seen Now!* is a treasure; each chapter is rich and satisfying. I came across one sentence that opened up a whole new world for me. As I continued reading I saw how each chapter continues the process of unfoldment. It really is a book on personal transformation. Like a rose that keeps opening, this is a book to savor and one I will return to often.
—Janice Campbell, author of *Practical Wisdom for Everyday Spirituality*

Be Seen Now! is a rich resource of unusual methods for those wanting to master public speaking in an authentic way. Using the information contained in this book is likely to cause the audience to perk up and perhaps even lean forward to fully take in what is being said!
—Kristin Morrison, business coach and
author of *30 Days to Start and Grow Your Business*

Through practical, transformative ideas and exercises, *Be Seen Now!* will help you discover your own vitality as a communicator and connect with the magnificence of your listeners.

—Justin Epstein, senior minister of The Unity Center of New York City and author of *Super You: 7 Steps to Profound Peace and Personal Power*

Lee Glickstein's tools in *Be Seen Now!* are impeccably orchestrated. This is the finest frequency evolution for both speaker and listener. This book is paramount for your speaking and listening future.

—Cheryl Scheurer, PhD, author of *Wealth Transformation: Integrity, Integrity, Integrity*

Within these chapters, Lee creates an internal environment of safety, science, and self-reflection for the reader. *Be Seen Now!* encourages speakers to:
- communicate with sincerity and clarity
- infuse their audience with a relational presence and genuine heartfelt awareness
- create a daily practice of love and kindness for self and others

I recommend this book for teachers, therapists, spiritual leaders, and professional speakers. An audience of 1 or 1000 would benefit from these lessons.

—Debra Joy Hart, TEDx speaker and author of *Grandma D's Bubbles: A Lesson in Life and Loss*

I recommend *Be Seen Now!* You will not just read it; you will keep it as a bible. Over thirty years ago, Lee Glickstein sparked my speaking abilities and lit a fire under me that allowed me to have confidence in myself even with a significant facial disfigurement. With that powerful starting point, I came to enjoy a speaking/performing/acting/comedy career for over a third of a century.

—David Roche, inspirational humorist and author of *The Church of 80% Sincerity* and *Standing at the Back Door of Happiness: And How I Unlocked It*

Be Seen Now!

Be Seen Now!

Inspiring Insights into Being a Fearless Speaker

Lee Glickstein

Founder of Speaking Circles International
and Author of *Be Heard Now!*
End Your Fear of Public Speaking Forever

PRECOCITY PRESS

*Dedicated to my late dad,
Morris Glickstein,
Grandfather of Speaking Circles,
who made my life work both
necessary and possible.*

Copyright © 2025 by Lee Glickstein
All rights reserved.

Editors: Rick Benzel and Julie Simpson
Cover Photographer: Jack Gescheidt
Cover Design: Susan Shankin
Book Design and Layout: Susan Shankin

Published by: Precocity Press, Los Angeles, CA

This book contains material protected under International and Federal Copyright Laws and Treaties. No part of this publication may be reproduced, distributed, or transmitted in any form or by any means, including photocopying, recording, or other electronic or mechanical methods, without the prior written permission of the author, except in the case of brief quotations embodied in critical reviews and certain other noncommercial uses permitted by copyright law. For permission requests, email the publisher at susan@precocitypress.com.

ISBN: 979-8-9909460-6-4 (Paperback)
ISBN: 979-8-9909460-7-1 (eBook)

Library of Congress Control Number: 2024919360
First edition printed in the United States of America

Contents

Introduction	xiii
PART 1: The Way of Relational Presence	1
1. Overview of the Relational Presence Approach	3
Bruce Elliott's Reflections	4
The Phenomenon of Brain Neuroplasticity	5
How Babies Learn Anxiety and Stress	7
Seven Stages from Fear to Freedom: The Roadmap	9
Don't "Just Be Yourself"	12
The Roots of Self-Consciousness	14
Use Your One-on-One Communication Skills with Groups	16
Come Into Your Right Mind	17
2. The Element of Listening	21
Receive the Available Listening	22
Cultivate Luminous Listening: Oxygen for the Psyche	24
Shed Light with Your Presence	25
See Others Through the Lens of Magnificence	27
Recognize Yourself as a Force of Nature	29

3. The Element of Gaze — 31

- What it Means to "See Your Listeners So They Feel Seen" — 32
- Break Down the Walls of Separation by Seeing Others — 33
- Sail the Sea of Faces — 35
- Provide Your Audience with Listening Eyes — 36
- The Need for "Mother Mirroring" — 38
- Understanding the "Father Gaze" — 40
- How to Hardwire Happiness — 41

4. The Element of Stillness — 45

- Develop Your Capacity to Share Stillness — 46
- Hold Me in Your Eyes — 47
- Be the Eye of the Storm — 48
- Meet the World at the Bottom of Your Breath — 49
- Speak from Dynamic Stillness — 50
- Come from Shared Stillness — 51
- Access a Sea of Calm — 54
- Find Your Sanctuary Within — 55
- Hold Stillness for Others — 56
- Being with Your Inner Deer — 58

5. The Element of Breath — 61

- Engage Attention Before You Say a Word — 62
- Be Easygoing in the Not Knowing — 63
- Breathe Easy — 64
- Practice Radical Authenticity — 66

6. The Element of Belonging — 69

Establish a "Field of Belonging" in a Room — 70
Liberate Your Eyes — 71
Accept that Public Speaking Anxiety Is the Norm — 73
The Anxious Person's Guide to Mindful Belonging — 74
Dissolve the Illusion of Separateness — 76
Be an Agent of Peace — 78
Practice Self-Kindness — 79
Soften Into the Moment — 80
Travel in Inner Space — 81

7. The Element of Silence — 85

The Listener-Friendly Pause — 86
"Hello Silence, My Old Friend" — 88
Your Presence Speaks Louder than Your Words — 90
Be a Provider of Quality Time — 91

8. The Element of Connection — 95

Radiate Kind Regard — 96
The Healing Energy of Natural Connection — 98
Realize the Paradox of Time — 99
Public Speaking as a Spiritual Path — 101
Save Time by Taking Time to Allow Connection — 102

PART 2. On Giving a Talk — 105

9. Developing Talk Content — 107

   From Katherine Kennedy's Book — 108
   Suggested Structure of an Effective Talk — 108
   Your Opening: Start with a Scene from Your Life — 109
   The Rest of Your Opening — 111
   What to Do After You Tell Your Story — 113
   The Body of Your Talk — 114
   Embracing Your Life Story — 116
   Tap into Your Rage to Contribute — 118
   On Being a Change Agent — 119
   Dare Greatly — 121
   Live Your Life Purpose Out Loud — 122
   Life Purpose Clarity Sessions — 123
   Befriend Your Inner Genius — 126
   Speak from Your Essential Knowing — 128
   Choose Presence — 130
   Find a Hidden Strength — 132
   Be Clutter-Free in Your Speaking — 134

10. Some Tips on Preparing to Speak — 137

   Find Heaven on Stage — 138
   Slow Down Time in Consciousness — 139
   See Public Speaking as Energy Transformation — 140
   Practice Vocal Freedom Play — 142
   Appreciate Being an Introvert — 143
   Facilitate a Soulful Space — 145

11. In the First Minutes of Your Talk — 147

- Take Your All-Important Opening Breath — 148
- "Let Go of Your Face" — 151
- Turn Your "Ums" into "Yums" — 152
- Heal Your Relationship with Audiences — 154
- Don't Look for Audience Approval — 156
- Tap Into Generosity of Spirit — 159

12. Maintaining Presence Throughout the Talk — 161

- Be an Audience Whisperer — 162
- Communicate Vertically — 163
- Practice Sustainable Communication — 165

13. Bringing Relational Presence into Everyday Life — 167

- Discussion Regarding Relational Presence — 168
- Words that Must Be Said — 168
- Let Muscle Memory Kick In — 170
- Parenting from Relational Presence — 172
- Parenting with Listening Eyes — 175
- Relational Presence in Parenting a Special Needs Child — 175
- Teaching from Connection — 178
- Rewire Your Brain for Self-Compassion — 181
- Relational Presence in Business — 183
- Relational Presence for the World — 185
- Applying Relational Presence to Language Learning — 185
- On Mastering a New Language — 187
- A Grandmother's Relational Presence — 188
- Relational Presence in Europe — 189

PART 3. Relational Presence in the Virtual World — 193

14. The Zoom Revolution — 195

Mastering Virtual Presence — 196
Format of a Virtual Speaking Circle — 197
Eye Muscle Memory on Zoom — 199
Zoom Circle Alchemy — 199
Vulnerable Leadership on Zoom — 201
Participants Reflect on Zoom Circles — 203

PART 4. Mirror Workplay — 207

15. Windows of the Soul — 209

Befriending the One in the Mirror — 210
The Mirror as a Portal to One's Lightness of Being — 210
General Guidelines for Mirror Workplay Exercises — 214
Face Your Mirror Anxiety — 216
Exercise: Greet Yourself — 217
Find Your Friend in the Mirror — 219
Exercise: See Yourself So You Feel Seen — 220
Commune with Yourself — 220
Exercise: Establish a Daily Practice — 222
Come from Powerful Tenderness — 222
Exercise: Commune with Your Goodness — 224
Laugh at Yourself and with Yourself — 224
Exercise: Let Go of Your Face — 225

Connecting with the Ancestors	226
Exercise: Mirror Meditation with a Grandparent	227
Flow Kind Eyes	228
Exercise: Radiate Self-Kindness	230
Be Impeccable with Your Word	230
Exercise: Level with Yourself	231
In Closing	232

APPENDIX — 233

Scientific Research Behind Relational Presence — 233

Relational Presence Improves Speaker Ease through Healing Attachment	233
Nervous System Resilience and Relational Presence Practice	242
Transforming Relational Trauma	245
Speaker Confidence & Audience Trust	253
Why "Open Focus" Mindset Works	260
Eye Gaze in Speaking Circles	263
Breathing in Speaking Circles	267
Essence Appreciations in Speaking Circles	269

For Further Reading — 273

Acknowledgments — 277

About the Author — 279

Introduction

Do you have a message you feel compelled to share with the world? Are you eager to spread the word by speaking about an idea that is close to your heart? If this is your calling, this book is for you. If you just want to overcome public speaking anxiety, you have also come to the right place.

As a teacher of public speaking over the past thirty years, it has become clear to me that a willingness to be oneself, and the capacity to do so, are key components of enlightened leadership and sustainable relationships. I have facilitated thousands of groups whose participants have discovered, through practice and receptive listening, *how to be seen and heard for who they truly are*. And being seen and heard for who you truly are is a precondition for fearless public speaking.

So let's talk about the universal fear of public speaking. When you consider answering your calling to share your message, do you find yourself beset with anxiety? Even panic-stricken? Perhaps it's not quite that daunting, but you just

To be yourself in a world that is constantly trying to make you something else is the greatest accomplishment.
—Ralph Waldo Emerson

want to get past some level of performance anxiety or stage fright.

Now, consider the possibility that your difficulty is not, at its root, around speaking. Consider that the actual source of the block is not so much the act of speaking, but rather a pattern of *not being seen and heard for who you truly are*. If this idea intrigues you, stick around and wade in. You are about to learn that this block can be removed, and painlessly, through the practice of *Relational Presence*.

The Kindness Curriculum

Be kind because everyone you'll ever meet is fighting a hard battle.
—Bob Dylan

We have innumerable opportunities to be seen and heard by others. The settings may be informal social events, structured work meetings, or high-stakes public appearances. This book is about how to transform these opportunities into a natural connection with groups of any size, assemblies of any composition, and even one-on-one. You might be a CEO talking to your team, a guest giving a toast at a wedding, or an entrepreneur making a pitch at a networking meeting. Perhaps you're a teacher welcoming an assortment of parents to Back-to-School Night, or a parent consoling your kid after a difficult setback. I'm sure you're already thinking of a time or times when you are called on to address others.

Although different in purpose and level of audience engagement, all these encounters have something in common: the tone that the speaker sets. "Kindness is the language which the deaf can hear and the blind can see," writes Christian

Nestell Bovee. Perhaps in initiating connection with an audience, it is the essential kindness that the speaker brings to the interaction that sets that all-important tone.

Over decades of facilitating authentic speaking, I have come to call this type of interactional kindness "relational presence." As this approach developed over time, it became clear to me that I have two main objectives. The first is to create a safe external environment in which speakers and their listeners can enjoy a deep sense of personal connection. My second goal is to guide speakers to develop the internal environment they need in order to discover how to be seen and heard for who they truly are—which is the key to becoming comfortable, fearless, and effective in front of any audience.

If you have been a student of public speaking, you've already been exposed to a whole host of tips, tricks, and performance techniques for engaging audiences. You've been advised to open with a provocative statement or an intriguing question. You've been shown how to gesture with your hands, vary your voice, and walk the stage. Although these measures can sometimes be useful in aiding speakers to "get through" a presentation, the relative success can often come at the expense of the speaker's emotional well-being and can leave the audience cold, having deprived them of true connection.

The practice of relational presence as a method of mastering public speaking is fundamentally different. In fact, it is precisely the deliberate *absence* of technique that uplifts the energy of the speaker and leads to an easeful and effective connection between the speaker and the audience.

> *Avoiding danger is no safer in the long run than outright exposure. The fearful are caught as often as the bold.*
>
> —Helen Keller

How I Created the Speaking Circles® Program

The easiest way to explain how I evolved the method of Relational Presence, as taught in my Speaking Circles® program, is to tell you about my background. Anyone who has suffered with speaking anxiety can likely relate to my origin story, which begins in a cloud of smoke, literally. You see, my mom smoked two packs of Pall Mall cigarettes a day, including the nine months she was pregnant with me. I was born with a buzz. Still have it. It shows up as kind of a haze around groups, a vague feeling of disconnection. For most of my life that buzz contributed to an undercurrent of anxiety and a growing sense of not belonging. Not belonging in my own body, in my family, in the world around me.

Growing up with what is now termed ADHD, back when such neurodivergent differences in children had yet to be identified, I was saddled with the folksy diagnosis of "ants in my pants." I spent my school days squirming in my seat and watching the big clock on the wall tick interminably slowly. My early public speaking experiences were in front of the family, around the dinner table, night after night, year after year, with a dad who alternately tuned me out or glared at me with daggers shooting from his eyes. My older brother regularly teased and ridiculed me, and my mom, the silent martyr, felt sorry for me. She too had to stifle her voice to survive. The sad part is that she was the brains of the family and its spiritual heart but had little voice in family decisions. It was as if we had elected the wrong president of the household and suffered mightily for it.

Like many of my "silent generation," I developed social strategies to get by and mask my feelings of alienation. But the one situation in which I had no strategies with which to control my fear was when I was thrust into the center of attention. In school I dreaded being called on. Giving a book report in front of the class was torture; with all eyes upon me I numbed out and froze.

I managed to graduate from Brooklyn College in 1965 by cramming for tests without integrating the content of my courses in any meaningful way. I didn't retain much information except for in the few courses in which the professor would occasionally meet my eyes for a sentence or two in a way that made me feel seen. Those few teachers showed me that there were learning environments in which I could sense connection, come alive, make a contribution. Looking back, what strikes me is how few teachers did that, and how little it would have taken to engage each student's attention.

I suffered from social anxiety well into my forties. Always feeling like a deer in the headlights when the center of attention, I settled for a low-key job in the social services bureaucracy. In 1974 I quit and moved from the "buzzy" environment of New York City to the calmer setting of Northern California. It was there that I began to confront my "deer in the headlights" syndrome through psychological and spiritual counseling.

Although I made progress in my mental and spiritual health, I was not able to break the terror of speaking in front of even small groups. But I had passion and humor to share with the world and was desperate to find a way out of my frustrating "prison of mind." Approaches that were built on technique and performance, such as those of Toastmasters International, just triggered my anxiety.

I felt called to devise a more natural way to move through this anxiety. After decades of trial and error I finally came to realize that I had been approaching the problem from the wrong direction! I'd assumed my issue was some kind of block in speaking that I needed to power through. The epiphany was that the problem was not a block in speaking, but a block in noticing and letting in the available capacity of the audience to hear me. This undoubtedly seems counterintuitive—that you, the speaker, need *to listen to the listening* of the audience—but it works. You will learn why and how in this book.

This shift in approach transformed my experience with groups and led to the formulation of what I came to call the elements of Relational Presence. Starting with groups of friends, I began sharing my understanding of this public speaking paradox; and, through word of mouth my methodology gradually attracted others. Realizing I had uncovered an actual business opportunity in addition to a personal calling, I devised the Speaking Circles protocol based on the elements of Relational Presence. Since 1993, facilitators trained and certified by Speaking Circles International have spread this transformative approach to eight countries in six languages, training thousands of people to become confident, fearless, effective speakers.

The Elements of Relational Presence

Martin Buber, in *I and Thou*, writes:

> *Our relationship lives in the space between us—it doesn't live in me or in you, or even in the dialog between the two of us—it lives in the space we live in together, and that space is sacred space.*

At Speaking Circles International, the sacred space Buber referred to is known as Relational Presence. It's the mindset we practice that informs our public expression. In a Speaking Circles session, participants take turns speaking (when words arise) and listening to each other, learning to be both authentic communicators and receptive audience members. This duality of roles reinforces the sense of relationship that is necessary to appreciate the full meaning of relational presence, the key to becoming a listener-friendly public speaker.

Whatever degree of anxiety you may have around fully accessing your voice, the cure is positive corrective experiences in an enriched listening environment. This experience of connection literally *rewires the brain*. My brain had essentially been wired in early childhood to trigger panic, and its byproduct, contraction, when all eyes were upon me. But the practice of relational presence builds powerful neuropathways that associate being seen with pleasure and expansion. (For precisely how this works, read chapter 1, The Phenomenon of Brain Neuroplasticity, page 5, and see the articles in the Appendix, Scientific Research Behind Relational Presence, page 233.)

> *Underneath the superficial self... there is another self. More really us than I.*
> —Alan Watts

Relational presence is made up of seven essential elements.

1. The Element of Listening

As listening is the powerful intelligence in the room, the primary guideline in relational presence practice is for the listeners. In the Speaking Circles protocol, the audience is guided to be available in a way that supports the person in front of the room to relax into that listening intelligence. *Once your priority up in front is to make the listening in the room more important than your speaking, a big shift happens.* With this new priority, the pace of your thinking and speaking naturally harmonizes with the listening in the room.

This same protocol works for both beginner and professional speakers because it goes to the common root cause of such public speaking ills as performance anxiety, self-consciousness, and diminished authenticity. It goes back to how we were listened to as children. Or not listened to. How our voice was valued, or not valued. As they begin to master this element of listening, many formerly nervous speakers find themselves flowing with ease as they speak.

2. The Element of Gaze

Whatever your content, when you face an audience in any situation your primary objective is to actually *see* them before you start talking to them. And to see them *while* you talk to them, staying for a sentence or two with each person. You don't have to get around to all of them; authentic connection just asks that you see the ones you look at in a way that makes them *feel seen*. A five-second "gaze of kind regard" as you speak gives the listener a potent hit of your relational essence, and the whole room feels it.

Seeing your listeners so they feel seen is a key element of magnetism and connection, so you will come across variations of that phrase several times on these pages.

3. The Element of Stillness

Our species is in its infancy as social beings. Or one might say, our toddlerhood. The expression "terrible 2000s" has been coined not only as a play on the idea of the "terrible twos" many parents of toddlers report experiencing, but also to acknowledge that the early couple of decades of this millennium, the 2000s, have been perceived as utterly chaotic. As polarization among humans in the world is tearing apart families, communities, and nations, many of us are finding mindful ways to soothe our savage nervous systems and move toward inner peace. In these *uh-oh!* times we need to seek our own counsel by locating an inner stillness from which we can listen to ourselves, our loved ones, and those we interact with. As public speakers, that includes our audiences.

We know far more than we think we know, and far less than some claim to know. But it is in stillness that this becomes apparent. "To the mind that is still, the whole universe surrenders," said the ancient Chinese philosopher Chuang Tzu.

4. The Element of Breath

Breathing in attunement with an audience slows and stills speedy minds, including your own.

If the speaker is not breathing easily, chances are neither is the audience. There are at least three opportunities to employ the element of breath. The most important breath is the one taken before saying a word. Another is after an important idea. Allow a long, leisurely breath in through the nose, stopping at the top for a few seconds, and letting it slowly out as you gaze around the room appreciating your audience. This lets them know it's okay for *them* to breathe. Taking a breath like this after making a significant point is the silent punctuation that allows the information to land and the group to feel connected to you and to each other. And when you get to a place where you are not sure what you will say next, a relaxing breath will help you think more clearly.

5. The Element of Belonging

Through these elements, the relationally present speaker facilitates a field of belonging in a room. With open ears and an open mind, the speaker is ready to share with the audience the experience of listening. With available eyes, the speaker sees those audience members as individuals, and with the breath, the speaker stills a jumpy mind and joins the listeners in the act of being present. They feel they belong in their chair, in their body, in this listening community.

Separation anxiety runs rampant in modern society, where epidemic polarization threatens nations and neighborhoods, families and couples. Holding forth in front of a group is a golden opportunity to bring people together in, at the very least, a shared learning environment. Your calm leadership can offer your listeners relief from daily anxieties as they find themselves in a field of belonging. Such a field has the power to soothe nervous systems.

6. The Element of Silence

In good personal relationships, whether in friendship, love, or therapy, natural silences arise, and some are golden. But with audiences, it takes a relationally present speaker to allow golden silences to show up. Such silences can let a point land and give the audience the time and space to process what they've heard. When you allow the psychic space that a natural pause provides, "public speaking" becomes a series of private communions. Silences may be perceived by some as dead air, but when they are allowed to happen organically, they foster a vibrancy.

7. The Element of Connection

Authentic connection with our audiences is our aim, but the way to bring this element in is by paying attention to the six previous elements. Any *overt effort to connect* results in a degree of *dis*connection, a false effort the audience can detect. In the language of relational presence, speakers *allow* or *invite* connection rather than *make* connection.

Similarly, we don't use the term *eye contact*, as it signals a forced technique that one *does*, a kind of *eye service* akin to the shallow meaning of *lip service*. Instead, we talk about a quality one *has*: the speaker offers *available* eyes or provides *listening* eyes. Authentic connection cannot be induced or cajoled. It simply happens when you allow your connection with yourself to turn inside out.

Organization of this Book

In 1996, I self-published *Be Heard Now! End Your Fear of Public Speaking Forever*, which was picked up by Broadway Books in 1998 for nationwide distribution. Since then, I've written hundreds of essays that transmit new insights and facets of my teaching and lifelong learning. I trust that the essays I chose for this book will bring warmth and a listener-friendly mindset into your speaking, and even into your daily conversations. The insights are intentionally varied and short. You can use the Table of Contents to dip into titles that call to you, and you might reflect on how each one relates to your capacity to speak in front of groups. I include stories and quotes from Speaking Circles participants whose lives in front of groups were transformed.

This book is divided into four parts, plus an appendix:

Part 1, The Way of Relational Presence, defines and elaborates on the various elements of the method. The intent of the essays in Part 1 is to both clarify the elements of relational presence and inspire you to incorporate them into your public practice.

Part 2, On Giving a Talk, offers insights into the phases of public speaking: prepping to give a speech, structuring a talk, and irresistibly opening a talk.

Part 3, The Zoom Revolution, is about the Zoom boom. When the global Covid-19 pandemic hit in 2020 we were compelled to find a way to bring the relational presence practice online. This seemed like a stopgap measure until lockdowns were lifted and we could get back to normal. But necessity being the mother of invention, in the ensuing years we have found ingenious ways to use technology to *transcend* technology. Even those who feel "totally Zoomed out" can calm their nerves and sharpen their public speaking skills in the "real world" without leaving their home or office. A great advantage of the Zoom Circles is that they include people from around the nation and the world. This part of the book is thus about the virtual application of relational presence practice such that the Zoom Speaking Circles experience has the feel of sitting cozily around the fireplace. Really!

Part 4, Mirror Workplay, offers essays and exercises that guide you in practicing "listening eyes" and fruitful self-talk in the privacy of your own mirror. If you feel called to dive into the deep end of the warm, safe pool of presence, you might start in the Mirror Workplay section (page 207), where you'll have the novel experience of affectionately gazing into your own eyes.

Appendix: I include an appendix that elaborates on scientific research around how the practice of relational presence rewires your brain for a better life, for connections of all kinds, not only for the art of public speaking. The articles in the Appendix are written by members of the Speaking Circles International leadership team.

Do It Yourself!

If the practice of relational presence speaks to you, it would be ideal if you could attend a professionally facilitated Speaking Circle in person if there is one in your area, or via Zoom from wherever you live. If those options are not available to you, I want you to know that *you can practice the principles of relational presence free of charge,* either with yourself in a mirror (aloud or silently), or with someone in your life willing to be a relational presence practice partner. To that end, after each essay you will be invited to do a two-minute exercise that will provide you with a real-life experience of the insight.

If you are inspired to create your own Relational Presence practice group, Speaking Circles International holds regular Zoom meetings (no fee) to discuss how to get a group started and how to sustain it. Email Lee at lee@speakingcircles.com for information.

PART 1

The Way of Relational Presence

1.

Overview of the Relational Presence Approach

I was never an extemporaneous speaker who could think on his feet... until with practice I learned to regard each student as an honored guest sitting in my living room, even if there were 300 of them.

—Bruce Elliott, instructor,
Lifelong Learning Institute

Bruce Elliott's Reflections

In 2002, at the age of 55, I retired from my business as a ceramic tile contractor to begin a second career as an educator. Having earned a master's degree and a PhD from the University of California at Berkeley, I was going to teach a course on British History for Berkeley's Lifelong Learning Institute. I'd never before given a lecture, so I searched the internet for a local class on public speaking and found Speaking Circles.

I immediately took to the Relational Presence approach and started my teaching career talking conversationally with one person at a time. Over a thousand classes and twenty-two years later, I have not deviated from this simple formula, which is so much fun and made me quite popular with the over-fifty crowd.

I've "lectured" at several universities on European Civilization from medieval times up to the French Revolution, dressed in character. I quickly developed the ability to stay with individuals without having to think about what I was going to say next. I had no notes. The words and stories would flow from my knowledge of the subject into the cozy relational intimacy I had established.

Without the jump start of Relational Presence, my teaching career would have had me lecturing like the others I had witnessed. I wouldn't have become an "edu-tainer" who often hears from students: "If I'd had a teacher like you in high school, I would have become a history major."

The Phenomenon of Brain Neuroplasticity

Brain research sheds light on the transformational impact of the relational presence approach to solving stage fright in front of groups and in everyday life. Neuroscientists report an almost unlimited potential for the physical rewiring of our brain, and we have found that such rewiring happens when a person with any level of public speaking anxiety systematically takes timed turns holding forth in front of a group of receptive listeners.

Where attention goes, neural firing flows, and neural connection grows.
—Daniel Siegel

The issue that brings so many people to relational presence practice (including myself as founder) is the triggering of anxiety and contraction while being the center of attention. For many, that response is a childhood survival mechanism that hardwired our brain to make associations that are detrimental to being able to stand in front of others and give a talk. That groove, that rut, was years in the making and decades in the maintaining. Patterns of neuro-association like these are challenging to reverse. The common approach of trying to overcome that conditioning with white-knuckle perseverance and a "fake it till you make it" mindset works for a few, but it leaves many of us moving through adulthood believing we somehow missed the boat.

However, you may not realize that the neuroplasticity of the brain provides a backup plan, a path of least resistance. Instead of the thankless task of trying to repair or overcome the hardened neuropathways, we have all this amorphous intelligent brain matter at hand that is able to form neuropathways with new associations that become stronger and more compelling than the hardwired ones. It's like building a freeway parallel to an old, rutted road, and this new route goes to a far better place.

The relational presence approach helps shift anxious thoughts to a fertile area of the brain, where the powerful new neuropathways you build associate being seen and heard with expansion and pleasure. Imagine the malleability of brain matter that allows it to be shaped and molded in any direction. Fifty billion brain cells, each a universe of its own, collectively form a million-dollar personal computer at your command.

This new association of speaking and pleasure develops even more quickly when we can clearly picture the mechanics of neuroplasticity and let it work its wonders on us. You can see neuroplasticity in action if you have ever improved at a skill, but then had a relapse and returned to your old habits. For example, if you have ever delivered a talk you were proud of, but then had a disaster in your next talk, it may feel like all is lost. But all that happened was that you got triggered and went down an old, hardwired tributary. Just understand that the old wiring is still active. Simply take a breath, find a pair of listening eyes, and switch over to the freeway. As the new pathway becomes more traveled, the old one becomes less available.

> **Invitation**—Take at least a minute in the mirror (aloud or silently), or in one-minute turns with a relational presence practice partner, to reflect on the pleasure of your own or each other's company.

How Babies Learn Anxiety and Stress

Pleasure is a feeling not commonly associated with public speaking. Recently published brain science research gets to the heart of why this is so. These new findings made me aware of how stressful the family learning environment was in which I first tried to express myself and was punished for it. As a result of that early distress, expressing myself coherently in certain situations is still a challenge for me.

We learn to attune with other humans through mutual gazing, usually starting with our mom or other significant caregiver around age four months. If this mother mirroring is not compromised by stress or depression on the part of the caregiver, the gazing is totally pleasurable for the infant. Then at around six months, it has been found, babies begin shifting their gaze to studying mouths when people talk to them. Thus begins the richly complex process of learning to speak. (An internet search on the phrase "lip-reading babies" will yield articles on the science of this.)

However, if the adults have not established a safe and comfortable environment through attuned gazing, the learning process is fraught with anxiety for the child. I refer here in particular to the language learning process. In the months it takes for the first words to emerge, and in the further months before sentences begin to form, speaking in this situation becomes neurologically coupled with stress. And even more problematic, the brain has wired itself for how the infant will approach all future learning.

If we want to help our children manage anxiety, we need to celebrate their bravery, not just their success.

—Krysten Taprell

Did you grow up in a dependably pleasant learning environment? With the best of intentions, how many parents are able to provide that in the world of hurt in which so many live? I'm sure I'm not the only one whose first communication teachers were a depressed mom and a rage-aholic dad.

And then the child goes to school. We humans are designed to learn best in an agreeable and even playful environment, but too many classrooms are anxiety mills that recreate the first "home school" experiences many of us had with our parents. It is common for a new participant at a Speaking Circle to be flowing along in good cheer in their turn and suddenly ask anxiously, "Is my time almost up?" I imagine that the person had a flashback to a very young age when they got constant negative messages about their worthiness to speak up in the family or the classroom.

Scott Hiegel, author of *Reaching Heaven on Earth: A Soul's Journey Home* (2022), wrote me this regarding his experience with relational presence:

> *I thought I had to talk fast because when I was a child, family members didn't listen attentively, and since what I said was often discounted, I learned not to say too much. I was frequently criticized and so I usually stayed silent instead of speaking my mind. And finally, in that penal colony called school, I had a fear that my mind would go blank when called upon, so I rarely raised my hand in class. Relational Presence practice taught me it was okay to be real and human and to make mistakes*

and that my voice was powerful. I learned it was okay to feel what I was feeling, to talk about what I was feeling in the moment, whether it was about being uncomfortable or afraid of the feeling of intimacy when gazing into another's eyes. It was safe to be who I was exactly in that moment, and I didn't need to be perfect.

> **Invitation**—Take at least a minute in the mirror (aloud or silently), or one-minute turns with a relational presence practice partner, to talk more slowly than usual about how it feels to talk slowly.

Seven Stages from Fear to Freedom: The Roadmap

Since 1993 I've worked with a range of people, from those with severe stage fright to well-paid speakers who want to have more magnetism. Ironically, sometimes these are the same people, since many professionals, concerned about being exposed, have managed to mask their trepidation.

As the practice of relational presence evolved, I identified a continuum of emotional states people generally experience when speaking in front of groups:

- **Terror.** The primal, animal impulse to flee from any public exposure, with little awareness of the source of this overwhelming instinct.

- **Fear.** This state is a step up from Terror since it is more possible to tolerate. The person has a sense of

Between stimulus and response there is a space. In that space is our power to choose our response. In our response lies our growth and our freedom.
—Viktor Frankl

what they want to avoid. A person in Fear likely has Terror flashbacks at times. At other times, in their better moments, the Fear deescalates into Anxiety.

- **Anxiety.** This state represents a positive step since it comes when the Fear has been faced and can abate. It is still an uneasy feeling, but it offers much potential to work with. Those in Anxiety regress to moments of Fear, and in their better moments find themselves Coping.

- **Coping.** This is the state where Anxiety is controllable but continues to lurk beneath the surface. Many people with significant speaking experience, even professionals putting on a good show, live much of their public lives at this level. Those in the Coping state revert to Anxiety at times, while often transcending to moments of Ease. However, once in Ease they often don't know how they got there. Or how to stay there.

- **Ease.** This is a plateau in which one feels pleasure and freedom in body, mind, and soul in front of groups, no matter when, no matter where. One who has achieved Ease has transcended Anxiety in public, feels in unity with audiences, and naturally facilitates a "field of belonging" in the room. When moments of Coping present themselves, they know exactly how to get back to Ease, which is a precursor to Flow.

- **Flow.** This is a state of soul-to-soul transmission that arises naturally from Ease. It is where movement and content emerge intuitively from the synergy of intelligence and emotion to inform, influence, and entertain. When Flow is intentionally developed toward a specific end, it brings Mastery.

- **Mastery.** This is the capacity to influence and transform individuals and groups in finite periods of time. It is the state of enlightened leadership in which visions become realized.

With or without relational presence practice, many speakers, including some who speak professionally, haven't gone beyond Coping in front of groups. They cope well enough to get the job done, but they're just not having much fun doing it, and neither are their listeners. If you want to be an inspiring speaker, this is not good enough.

Through relational presence practice, those who start in Fear—or even Terror—can move along the continuum to simple Anxiety and then to Coping. But the big breakthrough achievable through practice is the move from Coping to Ease. This brings you to the gateway to freedom—where pleasure shows up. When you begin to experience the pleasure of just being with an audience, the rest of the journey to freedom is a breeze.

That crucial shift from Coping to Ease arrives when you find yourself comfortable in the *not* knowing. This is most apparent when you come to the end of a sentence and are not sure what you will say next, but instead of having anxiety or a subtle contraction, you are perfectly fine taking an expansive breath while being curious about where you will go.

Shaping content is a complex challenge until you land firmly on the Ease plateau. But once you are there your content will arise more effortlessly, bringing about the possibility of Mastery in communicating essential knowledge in your specific area of passion.

Along the path described above, there may be some self-inflicted discomfort that needs to be tolerated rather than masked or run away from, so a willingness to learn from beginner's mind is an asset. When you can experience flowing with a group while in a state of not knowing, the pleasure of your own company has become a reality, and the road to freedom in front of groups has been paved.

> **Invitation**—Reflect on where you stand on the road from Fear to Freedom when it comes to public speaking. Take at least a minute in the mirror (aloud or silently), or one-minute turns with a relational presence practice partner, to reflect on it.

Don't "Just Be Yourself"

The exhortation to "just be yourself" or "be authentic" reminds me of the old joke about the fellow who asks the drug store clerk where he might find the talcum powder. "Walk this way," beckons the clerk. To which the man replies, "If I could walk that way, I wouldn't need talcum powder."

They told me to just act like myself. When I said, How do I do that? they said to just have fun with it, but I'm not sure what they meant.
—Steve Martin

You might think, *Well, if I could just be myself in front of groups, I wouldn't need your @!*$# advice!* But, in fact, my primary coaching is not "be yourself" but "be relational," *no matter how it feels.* When you are relational, your natural self comes through in a scintillating way that cannot be willed or calculated. To be relational with a group is to truly *be* with them, one at a time, no matter how large the group. This isn't just surface "eye contact," and there is no effort to connect or penetrate or otherwise grab attention.

Relational Presence is like improv for the heart and soul. There's no script...I'm not even telling a story—I am the story.

—Paula Friedland, counselor and life coach

Connection already lives among humans and is revealed when you neutrally allow communion with one person at a time. Most listeners will respond as iron filings to a magnet—and why a few do not respond is not your concern, so leave them be. When you practice this "muscle" of relational presence in front of an audience to where you feel pleasure in their company before you even say a word, and *while* you are speaking, they will sit in rapt attention as your unique self shows up in all its glory.

Want a taste of it right now?

> **Invitation**—Gaze into the mirror, or with your relational presence practice partner, and first "try to be yourself" for a half-minute or so. Then for the next half-minute or so, simply maintain a soft, steady gaze of kind regard with yourself in the mirror, or with your partner, without speaking. Reflect on the difference.

The Roots of Self-Consciousness

> *The only difference between self-awareness and self-consciousness is the judgement.*
> —Shellen Lubin

A passage from Jane Fonda's 2005 autobiography (*My Life So Far: Jane Fonda*) pinpoints the root of self-consciousness. She writes about her first child at age nine months:

> *It is late at night; I can't get Vanessa to sleep; I am despondent.... I am lying on my back on the floor, with Vanessa lying on my chest. She lifts her head and looks straight into my eyes for what seems like an eternity. I feel she is looking into my soul, that she knows me, that she is my conscience. I get scared and have to look away. I don't want to be known.*

This feeling rings like a common recurring scenario for those of us who grew up with self-consciousness. Some suffered the other extreme, where our gaze was returned aggressively. Likely most of us had some of both. Imagine reliving such a scene over and over again until the pain of not being met (or having our eye space invaded to meet the needs of another) brings us to a hiding place far behind our eyes. (As well, one can see how self-consciousness can be passed on generationally, as in the scene above between a self-conscious mother and her child whose need to be seen could not be met.)

Whether survival depended on shying away from attention or performing to meet expectations, our automatic behavior mechanisms kick in when all eyes are upon us. As a result, some are too terrified to cope at all in front of groups while others have developed a passable act, even a good act.

Though coming from different directions, neither state allows expansive presence. However, there is a way back to oneself from either extreme.

Here is what one Speaking Circles participant wrote to me:

What comes through in Relational Presence practice over the weeks is not the identity we were handed. With receptive listening we have the freedom to evolve our expression and be whoever we're going to be and that can change into whoever we are becoming—and it's OK to be in constant change. It's OK to not be consistent. It's whoever comes out to play in the moment.

We subconsciously put boundaries around what we're allowed to do and say to be totally free. Maybe the reality is you can be who you want to be in the moment, in any given circumstance. When you're self-conscious you want to be seen as acceptable, so you're trying to be that and talk like that rather than allowing your native creativity to come out and play.

The practice allows people who normally try to stay in the safe zone to get out of the box a little and stand for something.

> **Invitation**—Reflect on something you feel self-conscious about. Take at least a minute in the mirror (aloud or silently), or one-minute turns with a relational presence practice partner, to reflect on it.

The shift to relational presence is initially a challenge for many, but if you keep at it, you'll access that serene place where the stillness of relating to and being present with yourself and with another is pleasurable and nurturing. When you get there, see if you can allow words to arise without leaving that still place. When you stop retreating to your mind to figure it out or avert your eyes or make social signals like winks and smiles, you'll get a breathtaking glimpse of . . . yourself.

Use Your One-on-One Communication Skills with Groups

The great enemy of communication, we find, is the illusion of it.
—William H. Whyte

When I ask newcomers at a Speaking Circle what brings them there, most are able to look me in the eye and tell me what's not working for them with groups. When I ask how they are one-on-one, they acknowledge that's not generally a problem; and I can tell it's not by how they are conversing eye-to-eye with me.

It is then my pleasure to let them know that masterful public speaking is simply a series of one-on-one interactions, exactly as they are being with me right then, and that anyone with decent one-on-one skills can be a good speaker by simply applying these skills to a group. All it takes is practice in a supportive environment.

It's likely that over the years you've improved your one-on-one communication skills, but when you contemplate holding forth in public, that triggers anxiety. You're not alone. Many communicators assume that public speaking is a whole different animal from private conversation. It is not!

> **Invitation**—Reflect on the difference between your comfort level one-on-one and with groups. Take at least a minute in the mirror (aloud or silently), or one-minute turns with a relational presence practice partner, to reflect on it.

Come Into Your Right Mind

If you haven't seen the extraordinary TED Talk "My Stroke of Insight," by brain scientist Dr. Jill Bolte Taylor, please do. (Just search at ted.com for "My Stroke of Insight.") In the stroke Dr. Taylor suffered, the left hemisphere of her brain that thinks linearly and methodically went off-line, and all that remained was the expansive, present moment of the right hemisphere. Suddenly she found herself having a direct experience of the knowledge that "we are energy beings connected to one another through consciousness as one human family."

After recovering, she wanted to remember forever the beauty, the peacefulness, the truth of what she knew for those few hours. "So who are we?" she asks, and answers:

> *We are the life force power of the universe, with manual dexterity and two cognitive minds. And we have the power to choose, moment by moment, who and how we want to be in the world ... My left mind thinks of me as a fragile individual capable of losing my life. My right mind realizes that the essence of my being has eternal life. It knows that I am a part of a greater structure,*

To experience peace does not mean that your life is always blissful. It means that you are capable of tapping into a blissful state of mind amidst the normal chaos of a hectic life.
—Jill Bolte Taylor

an eternal flow of energy and molecules from which I cannot be separated; a part of the cosmic flow.

The practice of relational presence allows access to the part of our brain that doesn't recognize the illusion of separateness and allows us to communicate from natural connection. By putting one's priority on gently being with one listener at a time without even having to speak, the mind chatter and self-consciousness dissolve as the energy and delight of human connection expand to fill the room. In this oasis of belonging and unifying stillness, words arise naturally, lucidly reflecting our unique essence. We don't have to have a stroke to come into our right mind!

In her book *Whole Brain Living: The Anatomy of Choice and the Four Characters that Drive Our Life* (2021), Dr. Taylor writes that what she learned from her stroke experience is that we humans have "two cognitive minds." There is the non-dual, deep inner peace circuitry of our right hemisphere, where we are at one with the universe and nothing real can harm us, and the left hemisphere, where "I become a single individual . . . separate from the flow and separate from you. These are the 'we' inside of me, and we have the power to choose, moment by moment, which me to step into."

This implies that the conflicting inner voices that have plagued so many of us have a biological basis, and all we can aspire to is some measure of balance and peaceful coexistence between two wholly different minds. I know that most of us would like to spend a lot more (timeless) time in the right brain, which does not perceive separate minds but rather an ocean of mindfulness and luminous love. When we are in struggle, we may call on a skilled therapist, coach, spiritual guide, or good friend to deftly point us in the direction of that mind's wisdom.

That's the direction to which relational presence practice opens us. We access this wisdom by becoming mindful of receiving the available listening (discussed in chapter 2) in the listening field before speaking into it; when we do speak into it, it is from an attitude of inquiry, rather than spouting what we think we already know. A Speaking Circles participant told me: "I watched the videos of some turns and saw that I was giving myself my own best advice!" Yes, we become our own guru when we surrender to the shared stillness of a receptive listening field.

> **Invitation**—Take at least a minute in the mirror (aloud or silently), or one-minute turns eye-to-eye with your relational presence partner, to notice and reflect on "the two cognitive minds" discussed above.

2.

The Element of Listening

As a philanthropic advisor, it was my spacious listening that enabled my clients to powerfully articulate the social change they sought to advance in the world. More recently, I found that I was naturally able to extend the quality of my one-on-one listening to audiences of any size.

—Liz Sweet, leadership coach

Receive the Available Listening

As mentioned in the Introduction, the turning point in solving my own crippling stage fright came with the epiphany that the problem was not a block in speaking, but rather a block in receiving the "available listening." As a speaker, one must allow room to receive the audience's listening. Although it takes practice to do this, when you are able to do so, the audience's attention comes to you as if magnetized.

We have discussed how for those of us who were not seen nearly enough in our essential magnificence in early childhood, the challenges facing us in listening and speaking can linger for decades. It is difficult to let in the listening when you imagine it's not there—or worse, that those listening are judging you. But corrective emotional experiences of ideal listening can turn this around. In Speaking Circles, using relational presence, these experiences take place in a group composed of warm, intelligent humans who know what it means to "hold stillness" for another. Participants in these groups are people who are willing to become luminous listeners for others in their cohort, one individual at a time.

Quality attention by such a group creates a field of belonging that each person can explore in their turn. It is a safe place where one can discover, preach, inspire, inquire, try something new, tell a courageous story—or simply stand in silence and appreciate the luxurious stillness that others are happy to hold for you.

Feeling listened to and understood changes our physiology; being able to articulate a complex feeling, and having our feelings recognized, lights up our limbic brain and creates an "aha moment."

—Bessel van der Kolk

In an email about his experience with relational presence, linguistics professor Michael Rost wrote:

It blew my mind at a Speaking Circles workshop when Lee said, "Receive the available listening." It made absolutely no sense at first, but as I began to play with this idea during the workshop, it started to seep in. I didn't have to make demands on the listeners or strive to make the perfect connection. It was just being ready on my part to be open, observant, vulnerable, receptive: to receive what is available. That day turned my attitudes about public speaking upside down, and I've come to enjoy the opportunity to speak ever since.

In my decades solving stage fright and public speaking anxiety for others as well as myself, I've learned beyond a shadow of a doubt that receiving good listening is the key to meaningful transformation. And not only as it relates to public speaking; as a bonus, it is also the foundation for sustainable business and love relationships, good parenting, and enlightened leadership, to name only a few areas where receiving quality listening raises the quality of connection.

I was surprised how groups gravitate to me, as if by magic, when I tune into their listening.
— Mike Vogt, investment manager

> **Invitation**—Think about someone in your life who is a really good listener for you. Take at least a minute in the mirror (aloud or silently), or one-minute turns with your relational presence partner, to reflect on what that kind of listening does for you.

Cultivate Luminous Listening: Oxygen for the Psyche

Everyone shines, given the right lighting.
—Susan Cain

There is a finely calibrated vibration of receptivity to your audience that can vanquish public speaking anxiety. When I began treating people for stage fright thirty years ago, I didn't set out to teach about this vibration, this kryptonite to fear. Back then there was little nuance in my own listening. In refining my facilitation of the safest possible space in which to ease speaking anxiety—*to listen each other into existence*— I landed on a listening vibration that is palpable and at times intoxicating. This heightened resonance of listening is what you find in the best therapists, coaches, consultants, and other professionals; it is what makes true friends and loving partners.

It is also the same finely tuned vibration as mother mirroring. You will know what I'm referring to if you are one of those fortunate enough to have had ecstatic gazing festivals in your first year of infancy and/or as a parent. I had neither, so it's no wonder I developed a mechanism for getting it in my life by teaching it to others; in that way, I could create some great listening partners for myself.

Look at their eyes. If their eyes are shining, you know you're doing it.
—Benjamin Zander

We need this kind of luminous listening in our lives; it is like oxygen for the psyche. Getting this ideal listening from a friend, therapist, or anyone else lowers our defenses and allows us to think more clearly. Receiving it from an audience makes our thinking mega-clear. Such listening is the key to conflict resolution and the path to inner peace of mind. In business, it is the psychoactive element of team building and enlightened leadership communication.

So I have become an advocate for luminous listening in the world. I want it to be taught in school and become a staple of mindful parenting. Children suffer mightily without this kind of listening. (See Parenting from Relational Presence in chapter 13.) My passionate calling is to live life from this listening vibration and apply its alchemy to the challenge of speaking anxiety—and beyond. I want to spread it to all who still feel the illusion of separateness that makes raising their voice in public, and perhaps in private, feel dangerous. I want everyone to benefit from this oxygen for the psyche.

The key to gazing is stopping thought. Gazing is a soft focus; you are touching something with your luminosity.
—Frederick Lenz

> **Invitation**—Reflect on these questions in the mirror (aloud or silently), or with a relational presence partner, for as long as it takes to feel comfortable with the answers: From whom do you get luminous listening in your life? What are they doing or not doing that makes you feel truly heard? To whom do you give this kind of listening? To whom would you like to give it?

Shed Light with Your Presence

As we've seen, what dissolves performance anxiety is the practice of approaching public speaking more as a function of listening than of speaking. Luminous listening is marked by a soft, steady gaze of kind regard with the lights on behind the eyes. It is the alchemical core of relational presence and the key to masterful public speaking.

A dictionary definition indicates that "luminous" describes something emitting or reflecting light, something

Guided by my listeners, I eagerly go down paths I wouldn't otherwise explore. It's like panning for gold.
— Eric Atwood, executive coach

that glows. Luminous listening comes through the eyes more than through the ears. A twinkle in the eye can convey the moon without needing to be accompanied by a big smile. Luminous listening promotes an attunement with others that soothes nervous systems, especially our own. It makes us higher-functioning business and family leaders, and better friends.

In the role of either audience member or speaker at the center of attention, a luminous listener emits a gaze that makes others feel seen, that they too belong. Most humans crave that sense of belonging, and we can give it to each other through our listening eyes. In a roomful of luminous listeners, all transform, mend their minds, rock their souls.

Enlightened leaders are expansive listeners. Even fine actors lead with listening. In his early days as an actor, Alan Alda assumed that his main job was to figure out how to say his lines. But as he wrote in his 2005 memoir, *Never Have Your Dog Stuffed*:

> *"On M*A*S*H I began to understand that what I do in a scene is not as important as what happens between me and the other person. And listening is what lets it happen.... You have to listen so simply, so innocently, that the other person brings about a change in you that makes you say it and informs the way you say it."*

That you, the speaker, can listen to the audience as they listen to you may seem counterintuitive, but it is the fundamental shift that escorts you into fearless speaking.

> **Invitation**—Take at least half a minute in the mirror to silently provide a soft, steady gaze of kind regard for yourself, or thirty seconds with a relational presence partner and silently provide that gaze for each other.

See Others Through the Lens of Magnificence

Listening is the higher intelligence in the room. In my three decades facilitating Speaking Circles, it has been my experience that participants who submit to that higher intelligence reveal an irresistible magnificence about themselves. Magnificence is not about achievement, nor about being fascinating, though many attendees also have these attributes. Magnificence is an essential quality that comes in various flavors; for example: striking, splendid, noble, wise, awesome, masterly, inspiring, riveting, hilarious, transformational, heroic, elegant, eloquent, enchanting, soulful, expansive, courageous, luminous, passionate, radiant, vibrantly alive, and so on. (These are the kind of "essence appreciations" each participant receives at Speaking Circles after their longer turn.)

Let us remember that within us there is a palace of immense magnificence.
—Teresa of Avila

Many who come across at first as unimpressive eventually reveal remarkable qualities, which led me to conclude that humans are essentially magnificent. What it takes for those qualities to shine—in front of a group or one-on-one—is the kind of listening that allows expression from a place beyond intellect.

Every person you look at, you can see the universe in their eyes if you're really looking.
—George Carlin

This is why good therapists, coaches, friends, and partners become dowsing rods for awesomeness through their listening. It's also why many professional speakers who talk a great game don't show up as magnificent because they are delivering primarily from intellect, polished as their delivery might be.

At Speaking Circles, the audience is guided to listen luminously with a soft, steady gaze of kind regard while the person up front is asked to put full priority on receiving the gaze of one listener at a time and to speak when words naturally arise. As a result, when words come, they tend to be meaningful to the audience and often revelatory to the person expressing them.

So many of us find it difficult to believe how essentially awesome we truly are. In Speaking Circles, participants are provided with video of their turns up at the front; in this way they can see what the others see in them. The videos help counter a student's habit of assuming they were somehow lacking in their delivery. Over the years many have reported how viewing their videos changed their self-perception for the better.

I believe that gaining consciousness of our essential magnificence makes life easier in many realms. As a communicator, whether one-on-one or to a group, knowing the reality of your positive impact on people makes it easier to relax and come from a more soulfully attuned place, somewhere beyond intellect. Whether in friendship, in love, at work, or at play, knowing you don't have to put on a show in order to shine goes a long way toward being a valued communicator.

> **Invitation**—Take a minute in the mirror to notice an aspect of your magnificence and reflect on it (aloud or silently). Or take one-minute turns with your relational presence partner to reflect on an aspect of the other's magnificence and tell them about it.

Recognize Yourself as a Force of Nature

A weed demonstrates its strength by breaking through the smallest fissure in the cement sidewalk to reach out to the sun. We show our strength by dissolving the illusion of separateness between us and our audience.

It is the habitual feeling of separation—from each other and from creation—that causes so many of us to wall in our psyche so effectively that we are hindered from reaching our full expression. This illusion of separateness engenders self-consciousness and anxiety that has us pounding the walls with our heads (and minds?), trying to break free of a self-imposed prison of thought.

We have something to learn from weeds, which heed the call of the sun. A weed is not separate from the sun, nor the sidewalk, nor the fissures in the cement; it simply embraces the fissures and flows through them to emerge.

What is our equivalent of the sun that calls us forth as a force of nature? Here's my view. When we were infants, the eyes of one or both of our parents or caretakers were perhaps the unblocked sun: warm, bright, embracing, expansive, receptive, available. They reflected our integrity as a force of

Please remember that the lightning has never apologized for breaking skies open; the ocean has never said sorry for sinking ships. You, as well, must never apologize for being a force of nature.
—C. JoyBell C.

Relational Presence practice unleashed me into the world as a fully alive human blessed with contagious good humor and cheer.
—Bob Aucone, founder, Forum for Democracy USA

nature so we could express ourselves unselfconsciously into those safe eyes, and we could be silent into those eyes without repercussion. But as our personalities emerged, there came a time when dark clouds eclipsed the sun: scowls, disapproval, blame, shame, distraction, self-absorption. Many of us at some point lost our safe harbor, our true home, our spacious listening through the eyes of unconditional love. The disappearance of such listening is the genesis of self-consciousness and anxiety around speaking with and to others.

Meanwhile, underground, our wild weed nature unrelentingly still seeks listening eyes, our sun. Receptive listening is the prescription for wholeness, our channel to unselfconscious expression as a force of nature. Make a practice of offering regular uninterrupted listening to a friend or partner, or in a well-facilitated setting like a Speaking Circle. And don't take for granted the people in your life who give you special listening. Take every opportunity to appreciate them for letting you shine.

> **Invitation**—Think about someone in your life who lets you shine. Reflect in the mirror (aloud or silently), or in turns with your relational presence partner, about how that person does it.

3.

The Element of Gaze

As leader of a corporate team, I used to write my talks out and rehearse them word for word. Now I'm able to familiarize myself with the material and speak conversationally to the team, one person at a time. In this way, they really feel seen. Aside from saving tons of preparation time, I'm seen as a credible leader who doesn't fall back on company talking points.

—Butler Rondeno, team leader

What it Means to "See Your Listeners So They Feel Seen"

> *Only take someone's hand in a certain way, even look into their eyes in a certain way, and the world is changed forever.*
> —Iris Murdoch

When I have a Zoom chat with a prospective Speaking Circles participant, I ask what brings them to the program. Almost always it's about anxiety around public speaking. I let them know that I too am an anxious person, and to prove it, I sometimes show them what's left of my fingernails.

However, I also let them know that one thing I'm not anxious about is speaking to groups. You see, having lived forty-five years with paralyzing stage fright, I made it my second half of life's work to refine the art of seeing audience members so they feel seen while I'm speaking with them. As we have discussed in the previous chapters, that is the key to being at ease in front of groups, and of course it works equally well one-on-one.

The instruction to really see another person may seem impossible at first. You may wonder, *How can I really see them while I'm thinking about what to say?* Well, remember, as I wrote previously, the block isn't about speaking, it's about letting the audience see you so they can really hear you. So the work in the beginning is to discover how to see individuals so they feel seen—without figuring out what to say. When they feel seen, they can more easily hear what you have to say.

What does it mean to see a person so they feel seen? To answer this for yourself, you might practice with a loved one who reads this chapter. You'll both know it when you feel it. You can also practice with yourself in the mirror. (See the exercise below, as well as Part 4 of this book, "Mirror Workplay," for more on this.)

A speaker who holds the ideal of always being with one listener at a time so that they feel seen comes across as magnetic and relatable. And when this is your default mode of communication with groups and one-on-one, your words flow authentically, and connection happens naturally.

> **Invitation**—Take at least a minute in the mirror, in silence, seeing yourself so you feel seen. Or a minute with your relational presence partner seeing each other at the same time so you both feel seen.

Break Down the Walls of Separation by Seeing Others

Anxiety in front of groups can range from mild self-consciousness to terror; no matter its intensity, it is but a symptom of the illusion of separateness most of us grew up with and live with. Relational presence practice recreates a scenario that evokes that feeling of separation, but without the pressures of time or effort or performance, or even the need to speak. This allows the person to breathe, to "stop the world" and enjoy a relational gaze with one person at a time.

When humans are born, after our physiological and safety needs are met, our need for belonging is paramount, as per Abraham Maslow's theory of a hierarchy of needs. We come into this world as fully expressive bundles of divine energy, but as relational beings we need our divinity mirrored back in order for us to fulfill our unique expression on earth. We need soft gazes signifying: "I am here for you. I see you, I hear you. There is nothing to do, nothing to perform. You don't have to smile or delight me to keep me here. Just being with you and breathing together is my great pleasure."

The availability of such mirroring in our early years determines how strongly we sense that we belong—in our body, in our family, in the world—and how courageously and responsibly we will express ourselves as we grow. If this mirroring is unavailable or inadequate, the result can be fear and anxiety, rather than strength and fearlessness. The eyes of others become an unsafe resting place; we learn to avoid meeting another's eyes. With "the windows of our souls" boarded up, attempts to express ourselves clearly and have authentic relationships become complicated and compromised.

Such was my experience until the age of forty-five. Although psychotherapy and spiritual exploration gave me the intellectual understanding that I was not alone, and the capacity to cope and get by in the world, I continued to feel alienated within, despite having become good at acting as if I was doing just fine. In most places.

The place where I couldn't hold it together at all, though, was in front of a group, where I was frozen in fear. Looking back with self-compassion, I can see how that terror was a gift that helped me break down the walls of separation, as it led me to the practice of relational presence.

> **Invitation**—Consider the availability of a parent or caregiver's eyes when you were a child. Take at least a minute in the mirror (aloud or silently), or one-minute turns with your relational presence partner, to reflect on it.

Sail the Sea of Faces

At one of my Speaking Circles, a participant mentioned experiments cited on a PBS program about the brain suggesting that by the time they are nine minutes old, newborn humans prefer to look at faces more than anything else. Imagine that! Neuroscientists such as Richard Frackowiak have noted that the kinship that is vital for social interaction is communicated via the human face.

Wow! This notion inspired me to introduce a new slant at the beginning of the second round of turns at that Circle. Before I said a word, I took several gentle breaths while gazing at the radiant faces in front of me. From a place of childhood innocence, I saw each face not as a reflection of a personality but as a unique portal to our shared humanity. I told them what I was doing and what I was seeing, and in their turns, each of them took some breaths in that spirit.

On that day I saw how eyes come out to play when seen as a window to the soul rather than as a mirror or a wall. This may all sound mystical, but this perspective is actually the real-world key to success in business, in personal relationships,

Let there be spaces in your togetherness and let the winds of the heavens dance between you. Love one another but make not a bond of love: let it rather be a moving sea between the shores of your souls.

—Khalil Gibran

and in public speaking. Think of the people you admire, want to spend time with, do business with, refer others to, root for, or vote for. Think how they look at you, how they seem to see past the surface, into your essence.

There are those who can do this naturally. The rest of us can get there, though. To improve our relationships and mitigate our anxieties, we *need* to get there. And one way to do so is through the courage to show up and practice relational presence. Public speaking anxiety in all its varieties is but a symptom of objectifying the faces out there and not seeing the humans behind the faces. This anxiety can be dissolved with a subtle shift of attention. When you see one listener at a time with kind regard, you experience a refreshing and relaxing bond of kinship. When you then fold your content and structure into real world speaking situations, that human connection remains solidly at the core of your communication.

During a talk I connect with my body through breath while allowing connection with my listeners through gaze. These two elements keep me in the present moment.

—Bright Su,
improv therapist

> **Invitation**—Without speaking, take time in the mirror to recognize yourself as a unique portal to humanity; or with a relational presence partner, spend some time to see each other as unique portals to your shared humanity.

Provide Your Audience with Listening Eyes

When I guide speakers to maintain gentle eye availability approaching 100% of the time, I become painfully aware how in modern times our eyes are habitually averted, even among loved ones. Or when they are engaged, the eyes are sometimes

The soul that can speak through the eyes can also kiss with a gaze.
—Gustavo Adolfo Bécquer

used as weapons of judgment and a means of separation. It's a family history of averted or aggressive eyes that created performance anxiety for many of us in the first place. A key purpose of relational presence practice is thus to cultivate listening eyes.

I suggest that the gross underuse of the brain's capacity to attune to others is at the root of the miscommunication epidemic we see around us—in our communities, our businesses, our homes, in the world. The retina of the eye is part of the brain and is the visual gateway to attunement with other brains. While each brain is a galaxy unto itself, any two humans can attune and work together when the eyes allow it. This attunement requires—in moments of truth—a shared gaze where both are listening and neither grabs control. Rather, they remain *easygoing in the not knowing* while their brains and minds finely calibrate their natural synergy beyond personality and ego. (*Easygoing in the not knowing* means that you are comfortable even though you do not know what you will say. It is a phrase you will be seeing more of in this book, since it reflects a key leadership capacity.)

For those with eyesight, listening eyes are key to the essential human connection. (Many without eyesight develop compensatory workarounds that the sighted can learn from.) The nature of listening eyes can be perceived as a vibration that transmits the feeling of spacious receptivity. This vibration cannot be taught by technique or obtained through effort. It can be *caught* with pleasurable practice in a safe space with others who share the intention to be clearer and more listener friendly.

Seeing myself through the kind eyes of others reveals the truth of who I am and creates a kinder, gentler world on the inside and out.
—Jean Kathryn Carlson, Alchemy Life Coach

> **Invitation**—Speaking Circles has produced two five-minute videos, each with a variety of listening eyes, which can be used as a daily meditation. To find them, search YouTube for "Listening Eyes Meditation, Speaking Circles International."

The Need for "Mother Mirroring"

Only those who look with the eyes of children can lose themselves in the object of their wonder.

—Eberhard Arnold

The psychological term for where a healthy gaze is coming from is "attunement" (which can be seen as synonymous with relational presence). Gabor Maté, MD, described it this way in his book *Scattered Minds* (1999):

> *Attunement is a finely calibrated process requiring that the parent remain herself in a relatively non-stressed, non-anxious, non-depressed state of mind. Its clearest expression is the rapturous mutual gaze infant and mother direct at each other.*

At around four months of age, an infant begins fixating on the eyes of its mother or other primary caregiver. Over the next several months of mutual gazing interactions (or lack of them), the child takes on as its own the nature of the mother's attunement (or mis-attunement).

As the infant leads and the undistracted mother follows, they move together into relaxed, pleasurable spaces where the infant can interrupt eye contact without repercussion. This vibration of healthy attunement is precisely the same among mothers and babies in all societies in all history. This early training influences our strengths and limitations in being attuned and sharing emotional space with others for decades to come. A child with such a foundation has a great chance of growing up naturally at ease among others and fluid in emotional and creative expression.

But in our modern stressed-out world, many of us grew up learning attunement from distracted, anxious, and/or depressed caregivers. Aside from compromising our capacity for healthy attachment, this early training left us attunement-impaired in our own unique way, making us prone to self-consciousness and performance anxiety.

From our earliest days, our brain has been developing and hardwiring strategies for survival that are both a result and a determiner of the reality in which we grow up. If mom is depressed, the infant reads it from many cues, but most directly through her gaze. Its brain is hardwired to perceive that's the way the world is, and to strategize how to survive it. There is no faking it. If mom is pretending to be present but is distracted, the infant is not fooled.

Anthropologist Ashley Montagu posits that the newborn needs at least nine months of "womb" environment outside of the womb to mature. Many of us got the opposite of a womb environment. We picked up every stress and conflict in the household, spoken or not, and our brain developed accordingly. By age one, the loops and patterns and beliefs, both false and true, in our brain circuits were hardwired in. As indicated in chapter 1, relational presence practice can build new neural pathways in the brain that become more powerful than the ones bearing hardwired false beliefs. (See the section titled The Phenomenon of Brain Neuroplasticity, page 5.)

> **Invitation**—Without speaking, explore at least a half-minute gaze of healthy mother mirroring in the mirror, or together with a relational presence partner.

Understanding the "Father Gaze"

Mother mirroring, which an undistracted primary caregiver provides at birth, ideally kicks in for the infant at around age four months. The gaze conveys: *You are loved, you are safe, you belong.* The father gaze ideally kicks in when the toddler tries to accomplish something in the world of objects. It conveys: *You are remarkable. You can do it. I believe in you.* While mother mirroring provides a foundation of feeling safe and a sense of belonging, the father gaze speaks to a child's sense of efficacy in the world. Both impart self-confidence. (Note: mother mirroring and the father gaze may be provided by adults of any gender.)

How did your dad or father figure look at you? What did he see in you? How has that influenced your self-image? How has that impacted your relationships, your work, your leadership?

My first public speaking experiences were as a toddler at the dinner table, expressing myself with my limited vocabulary. On many nights, my early attempts to verbalize elicited daggers of contempt from my dad's eyes. I read in his gazes that I was a distraction of little value. This perspective dominated my self-image for many years. Internalizing his harsh gaze led

---

The master never seemed to have his fill of gazing at his firstborn child. "What do you want him to be when he grows up?" someone asked. "Outrageously happy," said the master.

—Anthony de Mello

to decades of stage fright. To be fair, my dad grew up during the Great Depression and heroically eked out a living under conditions more severe than I would ever face. The major stressors on him that caused the daggers I got had nothing to do with me. But a toddler has no historical perspective.

It is a challenge to overcome the messages of unworthiness that we internalized when this kind of father gaze was our experience in our early years. But we can rewire our brains by experiencing a different kind of gaze. This is where the practice of relational presence comes in. Learning to read positive regard in the eyes of others by repeated experiences with receptive listeners transforms how we let ourselves be seen in our essence. Such transformation carries over into aspects of our lives beyond speaking in front of groups. Reading positive regard in the eyes of those listening to us brings out our best, and in turn we can provide such positive regard back to them, thus bringing out *their* best.

> **Invitation**—Remember how your father or father figure looked at you. Take at least a minute in the mirror (aloud or silently), or one-minute turns with your relational presence partner, to reflect on it.

How to Hardwire Happiness

The corrective emotional experiences of relational presence practice can be said to rewire our brains, to "re-gaze" us, by building new neuropathways. These new neuropathways associate being seen with pleasure and expansion, rather than

By taking just a few extra seconds to stay with a positive experience—even the comfort in a single breath—you'll help turn a passing mental state into lasting neural structure.

—Rick Hanson

the anxiety and contraction many of us got wired with before we knew what hit us.

Having learned of the enormous plasticity of the brain, which is capable of new experiences at any age, I was excited to discover the book *Hardwiring Happiness* (2013) by neuropsychologist Rick Hanson, PhD. His elegantly simple method of using the brain's neuroplasticity to engender happiness mirrors the practice of relational presence, which I had developed a decade earlier. He writes:

> *This practice and the science behind it are neither positive thinking nor another program for manufacturing positive experiences, both of which are usually wasted on the brain. This is about transforming fleeting experiences into lasting improvements in your neural net worth.*

Invitation—You can experience this point of view with this exercise suggested by Rick Hanson: Look out a window or around the room and notice something with which you have a pleasurable association or memory. A tree, a bird, a photo, a book, anything. STOP and breathe for 15 seconds as you absorb and expand the sense of happiness engendered. Do that 10 times, or 100 times, a day and notice that it becomes second nature; the act of doing this actually builds new neuropathways in your brain that condition it to attract more happy thoughts and feelings.

The soft, steady gazes of kind regard and expansive listening we practice and experience at Speaking Circles gently move our focus into spacious appreciation of what already makes us happy. Rick Hanson's exercise, beyond providing fleeting good feelings, literally rewires our brain to attract more and more of the same.

4.

The Element of Stillness

When I stand in front of a group, I love the moment when silent stillness comes. Relational Presence practice has taught me a lot about myself. I used to wear masks when I spoke. Sharing stillness with audiences gently removed them. This has allowed genuine connection to arise. Public speaking has become a true joy.

—Tomasz Zawadzki, leadership coach and
Speaking Circles facilitator, Warsaw, Poland

Develop Your Capacity to Share Stillness

When your mind becomes still, your intelligence explodes.
—Jaggi Vasudev (Sadhguru)

As a newly minted octogenarian, life keeps giving me new beginnings. Like Grandma Moses, who famously first picked up a paintbrush at seventy-eight, I'm a very late bloomer. But one advantage of aging is that such new beginnings arise from the facts of time and experience. For example, my life's work facilitating unselfconscious self-expression has led me to the inexorable conclusion that everything good and sustainable between humans arises from a capacity to share stillness.

The capacity to share stillness is an energetic convergence of kindness; if this is not established at the core of a relationship, things inevitably go south as conversations meant to plan, brainstorm, or problem solve with one another bump up against the disconnection at the center.

To know yourself as the Being underneath the thinker, the stillness underneath the mental noise, the love and joy underneath the pain, is freedom, salvation, enlightenment.
—Eckhart Tolle

I find my personal stillness at the bottom of any breath, when I finish exhaling. I pause there for a few spacious seconds ... before breathing back in. Joining others in this space beyond words is the delight of shared stillness. Taking a leisurely breath together, along with a mutual gaze, is where essential human connection starts. In Speaking Circles and in life, our most meaningful content—along with our capacity to inspire, inform, and empathize—arises from shared stillness.

> **Invitation**—With whom in your life can you be comfortably silent? Take a minute in the mirror (aloud or silently), or one-minute turns with your relational presence partner, to reflect on what it's like to be with that person.

Hold Me in Your Eyes

Low-grade anxiety has been my constant companion throughout my life; even as I type this, I have a ball of Silly Putty on the desk that I work in my hand while thinking. I entered adulthood with social anxiety and acute stage fright. Extensive psychotherapy and spiritual work helped but couldn't exterminate the ants-in-my-pants of hyperactivity that went along with the anxieties and fears.

What I discovered thirty years ago that exploded Speaking Circles into the world was that, though I may not be able to hold a space of stillness for myself, I can hold a place of stillness for *you*. I know exactly how to stop, drop, and make my soft, steady gaze available to you, along with kind attention and no agenda. In service to you, my mind stops racing, and if you can hold that space for me, we can both relax into the warm bath of a co-meditative space of shared stillness.

That was my creative workaround that blossomed into Speaking Circles, where the listeners hold a receptive space of kind regard in quiet stillness for each other for finite periods of time. In this intoxicating field of belonging, one's anxiety with groups simply dissolves. Today I am far more at ease in front of groups (the more the merrier) than when I am alone, like now, in front of my computer screen kneading my Silly Putty. And in life, when I need good listening from a friend or my partner, I can ask them to please "hold me in your eyes."

You are never more essentially, more deeply yourself than when you are still.
—Eckhart Tolle

The body benefits from movement, and the mind benefits from stillness.
—Sakyong Mipham

I have learned to gaze into listeners' eyes so they feel like old friends, which allows my words to unfold organically and fearlessly.
—Amalia Starr, independent living coach

> **Invitation**—Think of someone in your life who has the capacity to hold you in their eyes. Take at least a minute in the mirror (aloud or silently), or one-minute turns with your relational presence partner, to reflect on how it feels to be listened to by that person.

Be the Eye of the Storm

When the Vietnamese peace activist and spiritual leader Thich Nhat Hanh passed away in 2022, some Speaking Circles participants reflected on how much he meant to them. One spoke of the Engaged Buddhism movement he pioneered, which held that our own personal awakening must extend to activism to be truly meaningful. Thich Nhat Hanh had convinced Dr. Martin Luther King, Jr. to take a strong stand against the Vietnam War, and Dr. King nominated him for a Nobel Peace Prize.

His influence on me through his writing was profound. This is from his book *Being Peace*:

> *In Vietnam there are many people who leave the country in small boats. Often the boats are caught in rough seas or storms, the people may panic, and boats may sink. But if even one person aboard can remain calm, lucid, knowing what to do and what not to do, he or she can help the boat survive. His or her expression—face, voice—communicates clarity and calmness, and people have trust in that person. They will listen to*

If you have the chance to be exposed to a loving, understanding environment where the seed of compassion, loving kindness, can be watered every day, then you become a more loving person.

—Thich Nhat Hanh

what he or she says. One such person can save the lives of many.

In moments of truth, when you place full priority on holding stillness for others, they breathe more freely, think more clearly, and act more compassionately. In front of a room, your calm is contagious, and the audience relaxes.

> **Invitation**—Think back to your childhood extended family and remember who was most likely to be the calm in the eye of the storm. Take at least a minute in the mirror (aloud or silently), or one-minute turns with your relational presence partner, to think about or talk about what that person did or didn't do to hold things together when storms would rage.

Meet the World at the Bottom of Your Breath

On the face of it, I'm the last person you'd expect to be a teacher and preacher of inner stillness. Anxiety has been my constant companion. My sanctuary has been Speaking Circles, where thirty years of relational presence practice has allowed me to facilitate inner stillness for others, and some for myself.

What makes this life-changing practice doable in daily life is that we have over 5,000 opportunities every waking day to plug into stillness for at least a few seconds. At the bottom of each breath is a natural resting place, where we can be still before we next inhale.

Breathe deeply, until sweet air extinguishes the burn of fear in your lungs and every breath is a beautiful refusal to become anything less than infinite.
—D. Antoinette Foy

> **Invitation**—If you are willing to go there now, take some full, easy breaths in through your nose and out through your mouth as you read this. Notice a peaceful place at the bottom of each breath, where your belly softens and stillness is all there is. See if you can rest in this place for 10 or 15 seconds before your next breath in. I'll wait.
>
> How long did you let the stillness last? Can you sense an opening to an expansive calm down there? That's your stillness center, and it's available to visit and nurture thousands of times a waking day. And when you notice and appreciate it, it can effortlessly expand to at least a minute. Go there when you think of it, and it will begin to call you when it wants attention.
>
> It might be said that inner stillness is a state we approach but never fully achieve until we pass into it with our last living breath. Until then, when we hold inner stillness as an ideal from which to enter any conversation (including inner dialogue with our self), we can drift/float/sail toward it on the wings of any breath. This lends a kinetic quality of dynamism to inner stillness. Rather than thinking of it as the absence of movement, you might think of it as the movement of presence.

Speak from Dynamic Stillness

The book *Dynamics of Stillness* (2023) by Ian Wright introduced me to new insights about stillness. One might assume that stillness is the opposite of dynamism, but inner stillness can be seen as abuzz with vital energy, from where anything can pop into existence. So when we meditate in *dynamic stillness*, Wright invites us to notice all the chatter going on and "not try to stop the noise." Instead, he suggests that we . . .

> . . . *actively allow it, letting your mind wander into the past, the future, onto thoughts, ideas, places, people, worries, fears, anticipations, whatever—but you must also do something very important, which is to maintain awareness of the quiet behind the chatter.*

As we practice noticing the vast stillness beyond the noise, we develop our capacity to simply observe our thoughts, feelings, impulses, while neither suppressing nor wholly identifying with them. Relational presence practice supports us to *speak* from dynamic stillness. When we share into receptive listening how life is for us, without "spinning" reality to make us look better or smarter, our vital, cohesive voice shows up. Wright's approach guides us in "tuning our senses to the great stillness," which, as he writes, "is ever present."

> **Invitation**—Close your eyes and take several easy breaths down into your sanctuary of inner stillness. See if you can sense into a buzz of dynamism down there. You might share what you find into the mirror (aloud or silently), or with your relational presence partner.

Stillness is not an icy lifeless world. On the contrary, stillness is bursting with potential and potency.
—Richard Rudd

As I drop into the stillness of the present moment, I expand into a field of infinite possibilities.
—Farina Chinoy, transformative coach

Come from Shared Stillness

November 2019 found me in Scotland leading four Speaking Circles, including one in Edinburgh with people who stammer

> *Within stillness is held unrecognized potential. Inherent in that which is quiet, still, and empty is the creative possibility of everything. All of the creativity that we experience arises out of that great mystery, that great stillness, that great void.*
> —Cheryl Haley

and another in Glasgow with speech therapists who work with people who stammer. All told, I worked with thirty attendees in that week, running the gamut from folks with severe public speaking anxiety to professional speakers wanting more charisma. At the fourth and final Circle, both these extremes were represented.

How could the same session serve such seemingly disparate needs? The answer came soft and clear in an epiphany on the day of the final Circle. That morning I had visited the Scottish National Portrait Gallery in Edinburgh. I was struck by the relaxing blanket of silence in the museum and the depth of stillness in the noble faces in the paintings. I could also sense the expansive stillness filling the room in which each portrait subject had sat, perhaps for hours, in many cases centuries ago. At one point the words *coming from stillness* washed over me, and it struck me that the inner stillness saturating my being was precisely the place where authentic connection and compelling content naturally arise at a well-facilitated Speaking Circle.

So I opened the Circle that afternoon by taking the time to breathe down into the stillness. I invited the others in the room to gently close their eyes and let gravity drop them down to join me in the shared calm. I had done variations of this opening before, but as a relaxation exercise rather than the key to the kingdom itself that I was now discovering.

With my newfound understanding of the seminal nature of coming from stillness, I asked the group to notice the relaxed neutrality of their faces and invited them to gently open their eyes and meet mine without leaving that easygoing stillness. After I took a long, leisurely breath from there with each of them, we had a short group discussion about how this felt and what "stillness" in this context meant to them. To my delight, they had their own words to describe what for each was an exhilarating experience. One said that she suddenly saw me as a long-lost brother, and another said he could not remember ever feeling so relaxed among strangers.

From there, it was easy to suggest that the work we'd be doing at the Circle would be to simply practice coming from this stillness, both as the person up in front of the room and as listeners in the audience. Nothing more, nothing less. No need to speak unless and until content would naturally arise from that space of shared stillness. As a result, every speaking practice turn—including those of previously hyper-anxious participants—flowed with grace and originality. The experienced speakers sensed no hierarchical disconnect from the others, since coming from stillness is the great equalizer.

This elegant dance of attuned mindfulness is the foundational key to the alchemical potency of these sessions and one that extends to all meaningful human interaction. If you sometimes have relaxed, attuned one-on-one conversations at work or with friends and family, you are already experienced at coming from stillness without having identified it as such. When you take the time to notice the element of calm neutrality at the core of your most satisfying conversations, you can intentionally bring that calm into challenging interactions. And with pleasurable practice, you can effortlessly bring your evolving capacity for shared stillness into groups of any size.

When you treat an audience luxuriously this way, they can hardly resist coming back for more.

> **Invitation**—Close your eyes and take several easy breaths down into your sanctuary of inner stillness. From there, see if you can sense that your stillness is shared with all other humans who are in this moment experiencing their own inner stillness. No need to talk about it.

Access a Sea of Calm

It's not always enough to go looking for the place we belong. Sometimes we need to make that place.
—Sangu Mandanna

I worked with a trauma relief specialist who was having difficulty developing a keynote talk about mindfulness. She told me she was working with an osteopath on Zoom toward rehabilitation of a broken arm that continued to cause her pain. She said the osteopath's soothing manner caused her to sense under the pain a "sea of calm" that gives her respite from the discomfort.

I was able to tell her something obvious to me but new to her, that the sea of calm she was experiencing with her osteopath is the same sea of calm into which she will be inviting her audience to join her as she talks about mindfulness. The qualities of the sea of calm are: stillness, kindness, peace, and patience. At some level we all have that still, calm space within that we can sometimes catch a sense of, perhaps through nature, music, spirituality, exercise, reading, meditation, and so on.

To access that still, calm place and invite others to join us, we don't need to be formal mindfulness practitioners. A few deep, easy breaths can bring us to an inner space where there is at least a semblance of stillness, a modicum of calm. This is the shared place that evokes a sense of belonging in our audience, as well as their best listening.

Accessing the sea of calm also plays a crucial role in business development. Business brainstorming and problem-solving often occur in the choppy waters on the surface, while deeper down there is calm. In *Catching the Big Fish*, David Lynch likens ideas to fish: "Little fish swim on the surface, but the big fish swim down below. If you can expand the container you're fishing in—your consciousness—you can catch bigger fish."

When I take a moment to rest at the bottom of a breath, I find a blissful pool of stillness awaiting me there.

—Laura Cutler,
psychotherapist

> **Invitation**—Close your eyes and take several easy breaths down into your inner stillness. Caress the area of your heart with your hands and see if you can sense into a deep sea of calm in your body. You might share what you find in the mirror (aloud or silently), or with your relational presence partner.

Find Your Sanctuary Within

I can trace the roots of my extreme stress around public speaking to growing up in a family that did not provide a safe space for me to be myself out loud. My parents followed the child-rearing advice of the time that a baby crying for no apparent reason was to be ignored so as not to "spoil" him. Speaking

Remember, the entrance door to the sanctuary is inside you.

—Rumi

Circles have brought thousands of worthy people into my life whose attempts at expression in childhood were stifled, sometimes mocked, as were mine. Over the years, many of us got relief through psycho-spiritual guidance that helped us find the semblance of a safe space within.

Mindfulness practices such as yoga and meditation are about accessing inner peace. The major role of helping professionals is to provide clients a place within to go to when under stress, a place where they can experience peace and safety.

Is not quality of life dependent on one's ability to drop into that sanctuary within, that place where all is okay no matter the circumstances? Imagine a billionaire whose mind is a dangerous zone of unrelenting self-judgment and critiques of others. Then imagine someone of limited means who has a peaceful refuge within. Who would you rather be?

> **Invitation**—Think of a person on the world stage who comes from extreme wealth and power, but who you sense is filled with self-loathing. See if you can find a place within where, despite your judgments, you feel a kernel of empathy for this person. You might share what you find into the mirror (aloud or silently), or with your relational presence partner.

Hold Stillness for Others

Antsy as I often am, my lifelong resistance to being still for myself has made me a squirmy meditator. But I found that when another person is speaking and my eyes are softly available to theirs, I can easily be still for *them*, no matter how many monkeys are chattering in my mind. Focusing my attention on the compelling space between us moves my thinking to the background and allows me to be still for another.

Being still for one another is the core of relational presence practice. It does not require inner serenity (though it leads to it). It does not require that we stop spinning our mental wheels (though it leads to that as well). All it asks is that we *be there* for the other in neutral receptivity and kind regard, no matter what else is going on with us. This is *relational* meditation, a *relational* stillness.

At first the practice may make you feel rigid, as if you were being asked to contract your mind and body. But as you soften your eyes and breathe into the communion, you find a spacious universe of flow within the stillness. As we be still for one another, we find freedom in the space between; we access the ecstasy of mutual being, co-mindfulness.

I've heard the objection raised that "only when I am present for myself can I then be present to others." But my overriding experience is that *when I am present with others, I can then be present to myself.* If this seems counterintuitive, remember that our sense of personal presence developed through being mirrored by others. If our mom or dad or other parental figure did not reflect our essential value back to us through their eyes, we may have eventually needed an army of therapists to step into that role. So you see, *relational presence came before personal presence in the first place.*

> *True intelligence operates silently. Stillness is where creativity and solutions to problems are found.*
> —Eckhart Tolle

I know how to be still for you so that time seems to slow down for you. Serving you in this way takes the focus off me. In front of a group, when I hold stillness for one person at a time I breathe freely and my words flow. The room relaxes. Neuroscientists would say that I am self-regulating my autonomic nervous system to reduce stress so I can focus on transmitting my message. As the group feels engaged, they mirror my autonomic state of calm, and we connect socially. Calm is contagious!

Holding stillness for your listeners is the most effective and pleasurable way to dissolve public (and private) speaking anxiety. And for experienced speakers, the simple capacity to hold nourishing stillness in a room shows up as magnetism.

> **Invitation**—Breathe luxuriously with yourself in the mirror and silently explore holding stillness for yourself for at least a minute. Or explore holding stillness for each other with your relational presence partner for at least a minute. You might follow up with a conversation in the mirror (aloud or silently), or with your partner, about how that was.

Being with Your Inner Deer

A participant at one of my Circles emailed afterward: "Each day I go out to see a deer near my house in the back field. In order to relate to the deer, I have to find that extremely calm stillness within. It is really a moment of magic as we link in."

What had struck her during the Circle was a growing sense of surprise that the same rules may work in addressing groups and in other business situations. Yes, indeed!

That's the place relational presence practice leads you to come from with groups of any size, or with any individual. Developing this "gateway muscle" to shared stillness drops you down, down, down to the roots of your full power of authentic expression. This happens because anxiety naturally dissolves in the room (and within you) as you meet your listeners with acceptance of their vulnerable depth.

When you are right in the heart of your still center, you are a person around whom real magic can happen.

—Richard Rudd

> **Invitation**—Imagine how still you would have to be to commune with a deer. Breathe down into that seemingly infinite depth of stillness and stay as long as you please. Put it on your calendar to be with your inner deer at least once a day.

5.

The Element of Breath

Breathing down through the layers of self-protection when held in the eyes of non-judgment, caring regard, and deep appreciation, I touch the field of Divine Love over and over and over again.

—Susan Kramer-Pope, artist and facilitator

Engage Attention Before You Say a Word

> *The breath is the bridge which connects life to consciousness.*
> —Thich Nhat Hanh

When you stand up in front of an audience to inform, influence, inspire, entertain, or motivate, your top priority is to engage attention, right? In conventional public speaking programs, it is commonly suggested that to do so you might open with a provocative statement or an intriguing question. I disagree.

To *authentically* engage an audience from the first moment requires giving up style and technique and returning to a beginner's mind. I strongly encourage you to practice the habit of taking at least one full breath, and maybe two or more, to land and establish your space before you speak. As you breathe, stay with a few individuals in the audience for few seconds each with a relaxed gaze of kind regard, seeing them so they feel seen. Without this opening, you'll tend to start the talk from your head instead of from your being. When that breath or two or three becomes your default opening, your talk *begins* in connection.

Here is an example. A vice president at a software company let me know about the first positive speaking appearance in her twenty-year career, influenced by her relational presence practice:

> *Presenting at a monthly national meeting, I did something I'd never done before. While being introduced I breathed deeply. My heartbeat slowed down; my nerves calmed. Before I spoke, I took another deep breath, looked around the room and at the participants on the Zoom screen. From there I felt engaged and connected*

throughout the talk. A co-worker told me, "That was the most comfortable I have ever seen you."

> **Invitation**—In the mirror or in turns with your relational presence partner, take the kind of full, easy breath you would take in front of an audience of 100 before saying a word.

Be Easygoing in the Not Knowing

In their first Speaking Circle turn in front of others, newcomers typically come to the end of a sentence and don't know what's next. You can see anxiety in their eyes as they scramble to think of something to say. This is a common place for "uhs" and "ums" to show up, or a few seconds of silent trepidation before they say something to "save" themselves. By their second or third Circle, however, you might see them experience some concern while taking a few seconds of silence and making their eyes available to one audience member at a time until words arise naturally.

After another few Circles, in the same situation, you would likely see them relaxing and breathing with ease and no concern about what to say next. The silence is comfortable for them and the others. Then, when content does arise, it tends to be more interesting and relational than when the person was coming from an anxious concern about what to say. Here's an email sent by participant Laura Cutler to Speaking Circles facilitator Lynne Velling in Los Angeles, shared with Laura's permission:

Life is about not knowing, having to change, taking the moment and making the best of it, without knowing what's going to happen next.

—Gilda Radner

I was part of a presentation team this morning in one of our regional offices. I usually like to know exactly what my role is in a presentation, to reduce my anxiety. This morning before we presented, I learned that my plan for the talk was not going to unfold the way I expected, and everything changed. I felt a slow, hot, anxious tension building in my solar plexus area. But I brought my attention to my breathing and after a few moments could see that this was a wonderful opportunity to practice "being easygoing in the not knowing." I was able to be internally flexible enough to go with the flow during the presentation, keeping in mind some structure about what I wanted to say, no matter what other presenters might do. I found that the "not knowing" made it easier for me to speak with one person at a time and even be available to speak extemporaneously in a deeper way than I had prepared. Words cannot begin to express the wonder and gratitude that I have for relational presence practice.

> **Invitation**—In the mirror (aloud or silently), or taking turns with your relational presence partner, reflect on what it might feel like to be easygoing in the not knowing in front of an audience. As a bonus, you might then reflect on how being easygoing in the not knowing would be useful in business and in personal relationships.

Breathe Easy

I open each Speaking Circle with a one-minute breathing meditation. I hadn't been aware of the scientific basis for this practice until I was referred to the book by James Nestor, *Breath: The New Science of a Lost Art* (2020), in which he reports that although we breathe in and out thousands of times a day, "humans as a species have lost the ability to breathe correctly, with grave consequences."

Many people develop the habit of chest breathing due to sensitivity about expanding the stomach. I spent my chubby, self-conscious childhood breathing shallowly through my chest and didn't start changing that pattern until I was in my late forties. Such patterns can bring on symptoms like fatigue, anxiety, depression, poor sleep, and stress. Making even slight adjustments to the way we inhale and exhale can jump-start athletic performance, rejuvenate internal organs, halt snoring, mitigate autoimmune disease, and, I would add, quell public speaking anxiety.

I once opened a Speaking Circles daylong workshop for ten participants with thirty seconds of each participant simply breathing with a partner in mutual kind regard, followed by group discussions about how that was for them, then another thirty seconds of breathing together. On one side of the room was a couple in their eighties who'd been married sixty years and had been attending Speaking Circles for seven years. He'd been a symphony musician, she a pioneering childbirth nurse. On the other side of the room were two young men who didn't know each other, one a software engineer attending his first Circle, the other a life coach attending his second.

What struck me in observing the two duos was that once the two young men were able to drop into what we call "a neutrally open place of not trying" in the second half-minute

Sometimes the most important thing in a whole day is the rest we take between two deep breaths.

—Etty Hillesum

I was an anxious speaker who couldn't control my shaking voice and knees. Fully utilizing my breath now calms my mind and body and allows the audience in.

—Sonja Rayne Lee, mindset coach and healer

exercise, the quality and texture of their shared presence was almost identical to that of the long-married couple.

Relational presence practice supports one's natural capacity to be instantly at ease with another—stranger or friend—without effort or judgment. Accessing this capacity may strike you as challenging enough in everyday interactions and especially daunting when speaking to a group, but we have found that in a safe environment it doesn't take long for most to recognize and welcome this easy capacity as an old friend.

And once you develop the habit of breathing easy with your listeners without jumping out of your skin, strangers become friends and speaking in public becomes a gentler game.

> **Invitation**—In the mirror or with your relational presence partner, take a minute to sense into the luxurious nature of doing nothing but simply breathing together.

Practice Radical Authenticity

There is no greater disability in society than the inability to see a person as more.
—Robert M. Hensel

I invite you to view a scintillating six-minute TEDx Talk, "Shelley Baer-The Beauty of Disability" (easily found on YouTube by searching on the title). If you can, take a look at it before reading further.

Shelley had never addressed an audience this size (nearly 500) and had spoken publicly about her disability only once, to a group of medical students. She prepared for this TEDx Talk by practicing relational presence at Speaking Circles in Florida.

When you view the talk, you'll notice Shelley's luminous authenticity. But what you won't see are the pangs of anxiety she was feeling up on stage. She got through those moments, she told me later, by taking a breath and holding her gaze on a listener till the end of a thought. Previously, fear in front of groups would cause her to speed up. She'd lose her grounding, along with connection to her listeners. "By taking that breath and staying with one person," she told me, "my mind slowed down to match my natural pace of speaking."

She respected her nervousness and breathed into it rather than covering it up through over-preparation and performance techniques. That's how Shelley transformed anxiety into excitement. I call this heightened state of presence "radical authenticity." Leaders, change agents, and visionary entrepreneurs recognize the value of authentic communication, and many have evolved techniques that simulate authenticity. But *radical authenticity* recognizes true authenticity as a relational process through which we create a field of genuine connection with our listeners in the moment, even when we are doing all the talking.

> **Invitation**—Reflect on what it might mean to transform anxiety into excitement. In the mirror (aloud or silently), or taking turns with your relational presence practice partner, start by feeling into an anxiety around public speaking, and exaggerate the feeling within you. Then breathe into that feeling and see if you can let it transform into excitement.

6.

The Element of Belonging

A large part of my speaking anxiety was an underlying dread of not being accepted by my audience. Discovering how to bring my own field of belonging with me and invite my listeners into it changed everything.

—Audrey Seymour, founder,
Clear Change Group

I didn't belong as a kid, and that always bothered me. If only I'd known that one day my differentness would be an asset, then my early life would have been much easier.

—Bette Midler

Establish a "Field of Belonging" in a Room

Indigenous peoples maintain continuous physical contact with infants until they begin crawling on their own impulse, usually at six to eight months. Then the mom or dad carries the child on their back into the field or other work area, thus involving them in adult endeavors. As a result, these children grow up without self-consciousness, feeling absolutely at home in their bodies and in their tribe. Belonging is the *assumption*.

By contrast, in modern Western society we are often separated from our parents. We sleep alone, isolated, and perhaps subject to parenting techniques and controls that undermine our natural learning process. As a result, the sense of alienation and not belonging is epidemic, and so pervasive we are hardly aware of it. This profound sense of not belonging kicks in big time when we face a group, which is why so many of us are beset by performance anxiety.

The good news is that when we become aware of this dynamic and realize that most of our listeners are craving to belong, even though it is not apparent in their demeanor, we have the power to place our first and ongoing priority on allowing them to belong. We give them an instant doorway to belonging—with our listening eyes before we speak and while we speak. This takes the focus off of us and places it onto serving them. And by giving *them* the space to belong, *we* belong.

This is a challenge for many speakers because of our own discomfort with silence. The need to *do something* kicks in precisely when we are the center of attention. But until we know in our bones how to guide our audience to feel at home in their bodies and in the room, their attention will wander, and our anxiety will do its thing, thus perpetuating a feeling of separateness.

Relational presence practice is a way out of that loop, a path to mastering your natural capacity to be with a group of any size, one person at a time, seeing them so they feel seen. As you establish a "field of belonging" for your audience, you are on your way to becoming a masterful communicator, one who can facilitate belonging in a world that fosters the illusion of separateness.

My sense of belonging broke down barriers, relaxed and excited me so my words would just tumble out.
— Susan Amanda Schratter, marriage and family therapist

> **Invitation**—Recall a time in your life when you felt you absolutely didn't belong, whether in your family, your class at school, or in a social group. In the mirror (aloud or silently), or taking turns with your relational presence partner, remember how that felt, and perhaps reflect on it.

Liberate Your Eyes

The indigenous peoples mentioned in the previous essay have no need to meet eyes to feel connected and would likely see our emphasis on the eye gaze as strange and unnatural. But many of us in modern Western society have developed lifetime habits of grasping, signaling, pleasing, controlling, or deferring with our eyes.

There is a difference between running with all your heart with your eyes closed and running with all your heart with your eyes wide open.
—Simon Sinek

As infants our eyes were naturally wide open to the world around us, especially to the people closest to us. But overwhelmed with the pressures of life, these intimates let us know—explicitly or reactively—that remaining wide open isn't safe in this world. There is practical usefulness in this caution, but for survival we gave up a lot of our natural sense of connection with other humans. And along the way, we likely had other people's anger, blame, shame, or sadness injected into our being through our innocent eyes.

We learned that it wasn't safe to keep our eyes available to strangers, and sometimes even those closest to us, so we drew the shades and developed subtle strategies to hide our hearts; we dared not look out boldly from the center of our beings with the wonder and awe of the adventurers we were born to be. Many of us either developed patterns of self-consciousness to avoid attention at all costs, or compensated by grabbing attention at every opportunity, or some of each. These reactive mindsets blocked us from meeting the profound need for authentic connection.

So here we are, up against the brick wall of this modern epidemic of so many craving to belong and not knowing how to have that happen. That's your audience. To facilitate a "field of belonging" to meet their deepest need and thus draw their attention and best listening, you first want to liberate your eyes and invite your audience in. In doing so, you will practice nothing less than the wizardry of dissolving their illusion of separateness.

> **Invitation**—In the mirror or with your relational presence partner, take a minute to share a soft, steady gaze of kind regard.

Accept that Public Speaking Anxiety Is the Norm

Humans are herd animals. Our brains are hardwired to assume that if separated from the herd we will not survive. When a sea of eyes provokes in us those feelings of separation, our normal coping mechanisms become useless. We experience a primal fear for our survival. The neocortex—the rational part of the brain that knows we are not in danger—shuts down, while the reptile brain takes over, preparing us to flee, fight, or freeze. Feel familiar?

Such stress—and the shame around it—has led many an otherwise naturally capable person to adopt coping strategies to mask or conquer the anxiety. But such strategies interfere with quality communication, and when we sense that, the result is more anxiety. The way out of this unhappy cycle is to first understand that performance anxiety is normal, and that it is possible to work through.

Through relational presence practice, the illusion of separateness dissolves. We find we are able to communicate to groups from *within* the herd. The title of my previous book, *Be Heard Now!*, might just as aptly have been *Be Herd Now!*

I would love to work on Broadway, but I don't know that it would manifest itself in musical theater. I have terrible stage fright that I'd have to get over.
—Scarlett Johannson

The Anxious Person's Guide to Mindful Belonging

Gazing at the rain, I consider what it means to belong, to become part of something. To have someone cry for me.
—Haruki Murakami

I have been searching for peace of mind all my life. When the practice of Transcendental Meditation was popular fifty years ago, I bombed out. Back then you were to bring a flower as an offering to the teacher at the first meeting. On the way to my first TM session, I pulled out from the ground a scrawny specimen alongside the highway. Sure, it had a blossom on it but for all I knew, it was a weed. The teacher looked at it and at me with disdain. Bad start. I still remember my TM mantra and when I thought of it just now, I started to bite my nails.

At one point I was in a psycho-spiritual program that met one weekend a month. Each day opened with a twenty-minute meditation. Picture two hundred of us *Om*-ing into divine stillness. Though it afforded some relaxation, I often had the sense I wasn't doing it right and found myself just biding time until I could stand up and walk the hell out. In four years with the program, I never felt the comfort of *Om*.

In Canada for a ten-day silent Vipassana retreat, I cheated with a couple of other outlaws. After a private consult with the teacher who worked with me to focus on feeling the breath under my nose, it took me only five minutes on my own to

> **Invitation**—Reflect on how you sometimes mask your anxiety in life situations. Reflect on that in the mirror (aloud or silently), or take turns reflecting on it with your relational presence partner.

give up and white knuckle it until a break, when I could meet "behind the barn" with fellow conspirators to whisper our discontents.

At meditation workshops and several Satsang evenings, I thought I got it and vowed to continue a daily practice, but that vow never lasted longer than a diet starting the first of January. Over the years I've tried guided meditations with masters through audio programs and YouTube videos. Wonderful stuff but . . . always I experienced the same incapacity or unwillingness to sustain. I even tried meditating with my spiritually attuned wife, but I couldn't turn off the inner voice telling me how very "less than" I was. Divorce was predictable.

As the idea of inner peace has always resonated with me, and considering all the wisdom out there about the transformational nature of stillness, I thought something was wrong with me for not being able to "get there." With my checkered track record, I couldn't imagine that I'd be expanding to daily twenty-minute meditation experiences anytime soon.

It was clear I'd have to devise my own practice, one that would actually be effortless. With no expectations for quick results, or any results at all, I started exploring a new path of "meditation lite," and finally experienced a homecoming.

As I was engaged in a simple routine of mindful breathing, I noticed a natural pause between the end of an exhale and the beginning of the next inhale. Sitting or reclining, eyes open or closed, at the bottom of each full breath there were a few seconds of rest that gradually expanded to ten or fifteen seconds. With practice to linger in that pause, I would feel the pleasure of its stillness and could easily extend it for thirty seconds, and eventually to a minute.

I allow each sweet breath, as it comes in and goes out, to make its unique, nuanced, round trip through my body and being. In this free-flowing adventure, I find myself playing with my breath as it curls through my body and my being and finds stillness in the darnedest places. Sometimes it feels like an inner amusement park ride. Expanding your inner sanctuary through any kind of meditation practice is good and can be quite enough. It can assist in all aspects of your life. If you are on a leadership track, the practice of dropping into and coming from stillness with a group is an excellent way to pierce through the illusion of separateness.

> **Invitation**—In the mirror (aloud or silently), or taking turns with your relational presence partner, reflect on your history around meditation practice.

Dissolve the Illusion of Separateness

The fundamental delusion of humanity is to suppose that I am here and you are out there.
—Hakuun Yasutani

Anxiety and contraction in front of groups are consequences of the illusion of separateness, which is endemic in our modern world. Performance technique, guile, and over-preparation are commonly employed to cope with audiences when one assumes a me/them polarity, but most of us just don't have it in us to "put on a show." The path of least resistance starts with realizing that just about everyone out there, no matter how they appear to have it together, is also laboring under the illusion of separateness. Most anyone not raised in a functional family has a deep, largely unmet, yearning for community.

Knowing this enables you to shift focus from your own feelings of being separate up there in front of the room, to facilitating a field of belonging for your audience. Once you are able to do this, anxiety releases and life naturally expresses through you. By providing your listeners with a field of belonging through the practice of relational presence, you dissolve the illusion of separateness for *yourself* as well as for your listeners. You bring out the best in your audience, while they evoke the best in you.

Pam Noda, Speaking Circles facilitator in Tokyo, wrote:

> *The audience was laughing, nodding heads, smiling, making me feel like I belonged in front of them as I talked about something dear to all our hearts. But what they were giving me, I had given them first. By taking the time to breathe, gaze into eyes individually, and see them as a group before I began to speak, I had let them know, "You belong."*

Feeling into the reality that I and my listeners are one erased self-judgment and took me from fear to love.
—Johanna Derbolowsky, transformation coach

A human being ... experiences himself, his thoughts and feelings, as something separate from the rest—a kind of optical illusion of consciousness. This delusion is a kind of prison for us, restricting us to our personal desires and affection for a few persons nearest to us.
—Albert Einstein

> **Invitation**—Reflect on how you sometimes feel completely separate from others. In the mirror (aloud or silently), or taking turns with your relational presence partner, try on the possibility that at those times you are having a kind of optical illusion of disconnection.

Be an Agent of Peace

> *It is better to have peace of mind than piece of land.*
> —Mark Samraj

Recently I heard a radio ad for a cable TV service that trumpeted peace of mind as its promise. "And isn't it all about peace of mind?" were the closing words. In the next few days I heard the phrase twice more, in ads for a bank and for a car. It may sound trite, but . . . *isn't that what it's all about?*

A Speaking Circles participant talked about his mind going crazy about money. He couldn't stop catastrophizing until he met with a financial advisor whose kind manner and expertise soothed his nervous system; he could breathe again and think clearly around money. We sometimes need other intelligent life to listen well to our stress and normalize it. That's what great friends do and what therapists are paid for.

Speaking Circles participants often share about their peace of mind or lack of it, or their sense of belonging or of being an outsider. The kind listening eyes they speak into in the Circle hold a safe space for deeper inquiry into what would be useful to know right now. In community we can all relate to each other's joys and tribulations. In certain aspects of life, when my wild mind is embattled, I need agents of peace to raise me up through listening. And in my area of expertise around performance anxiety in all its forms, my life's work is to be an agent of inner peace for others. Relational presence practice offers this to you as well.

> **Invitation**—Who is an agent of peace for you, and for whom are you an agent of peace? Reflect on that in the mirror or take turns with your partner.

Practice Self-Kindness

The early years of the Covid-19 global pandemic, which I refer to as the "Covid times," became for me a sanctuary for clear thinking. Along the way I learned that crystal clarity can sometimes be hard to accept when it points to something that must be changed yet I can't imagine how. For instance . . . one day out of nowhere a clear inner voice told me in no uncertain terms: *It's time for you to be kind to yourself!* Well, that got my attention. I hardly ever experience a clear inner voice, and I had no idea I was not being kind to myself. But after a couple of deep breaths, I realized how regularly I treat myself with unkind regard. Like off and on all day.

This negativity doesn't come in the form of any overt self-talk telling me what's wrong with me. Rather, it's just a vague, recurrent undertone of unhappiness with myself, like I don't belong in this world. On my way to becoming clearer about this, I found myself writing to myself: *NOW is the time to be kind to myself. Get off my own back, sweet man. Be as gentle to myself as I am to other humanoids who cross my path.*

How does one be kind to oneself? If your inner critic is as active as mine, the opportunity arises many times a day to catch yourself giving self-messages to which you would never subject a loved one. When we catch it, we can take a deep breath and stop the abuse in the moment. That opens up some space to replace the negative self-talk with a thought or phrase containing a message of kindness instead. Some of the most inspiring Speaking Circles turns I have seen exhibit elements of the dawning of self-kindness, where a habit of

You have been criticizing yourself for years, and it hasn't worked. Try approving of yourself and see what happens.

—Louise Hay

What I learned in this practice was that I did not have to agree with that inner voice saying, "I am not enough." I could instead simply show up for an audience being enough.

—Sandra Shurtz, life coach

unkind self-regard comes to light and, through that awareness, begins to dissolve.

> **Invitation**—Think about where you are on a self-kindness scale of one to ten, with one being "I am hardly ever kind to myself" and ten being "I am always kind to myself." Reflect on the extent of your self-kindness in the mirror (aloud or silently), or by talking about it in turns with your relational presence partner.

Soften Into the Moment

whatever you do
be gentle with yourself.
you don't just live
in this world
or your home
or your skin.
you also live
in someone's eyes.
—Sanober Khan, poet

At a Speaking Circles facilitator training, my training partner Doreen Downing invited one of our trainees to "soften into the moment." My body, with which I am not often in good communication, instantly sighed YES! and I too softened into the moment as I observed. *Soften into the moment* became a mantra for me. Those words bring me to a special place, a sweet spot from where I want all my communications to arise. I soften into the moment, and then into the next moment, and the next and the next, until I am softening into the river of life... softening into compassion for all humanity. This profound sense of belonging is from where masterful communication arises.

The great communicators come from this place. Effective business leaders build trust and loyalty from here. And softening into the moment is a fundamental parenting and relationship skill that can defuse a power struggle. Once you intellectually grasp this foundational reality, it yields results when practiced without effort. When you tap into the ease of softening into the listening rather than hardening into an attitude or a script, connection arises.

You may think of the "moment" as a river. Anxiety and contraction around public speaking are the products of habitually trying to swim/speak against the current. Once you get a taste of softening into the river of listening, your connection with audiences changes forever.

> **Invitation**—In the mirror or with your relational presence partner, without speaking, experience what it feels like to "soften into the moment," and into the next moment, and so on, for as long as it feels comfortable.

Travel in Inner Space

The phrase "outer space" points to the infinite expanse beyond our planet, beyond our solar system. You won't find many folks who deny the notion of outer space, but what of the notion that this vast outer space is echoed within us by a vast inner space?

The cosmos is within us. We are made of star-stuff. We are a way for the universe to know itself.
—Carl Sagan

Whether due to early childhood trauma, genetic neuroatypicality, or a combination of factors, my inner space consciousness was extremely limited. Despite exposure to modalities designed to expand that realm (meditation, breathwork, spiritual practices), I often remained stranded on the launching pad when it came to solo inner space travel.

But I discovered that I can find spaciousness and a sense of belonging within when I am witnessed and listened to by conscious others. And this is why my soul's calling was to "invent" relational presence practice and become a practitioner of it.

John Kinyon's profound state of self-compassion through inner space travel was cultivated through years of Nonviolent Communication practice. He became a teacher of NVC, worked closely with its founder, Marshall Rosenberg, and developed the international training program *Mediate Your Life*. He came to Speaking Circles to help bring his self-compassion into leadership speaking via relational presence. How is this done? John wrote this to me and gave me permission to share it here:

Relational Presence creates awareness of an inexhaustible internal source of personal wisdom that is always available.
—Christoph Van Doninck, customer experience specialist

> *The expansive group listening welcomes and amplifies the experience of safety within us. The safe space within is always available. I often lose touch with it but it's always something I have the potential to come back to over and over again. Peace and joy are already in this space, and the experience of love and beauty. I can find these qualities within that aren't dependent on external conditions being a certain way. From there I can engage with the world in a way that brings more satisfaction, meaning and purpose. When I can consciously breathe and feel into that place where I already know I'm safe in the present moment, I can create empathic connection within me, and with audiences.*

Invitation—In the mirror or in turns with your relational presence partner, take 30 seconds or so to sense into the vastness of outer space. Then reflect on the notion that your inner space is just as vast and see where that takes you in the next 30 seconds or longer.

7.

The Element of Silence

I envied how some Speaking Circles participants transitioned between thoughts with a relaxed, silent breath that lured me in. When I was up front completing a thought, I was anxious about where to go next. But when I stopped to breathe, to be present with my listeners, I felt the powerful anticipation of "Oh, my gosh! What's coming next?" Now my curiosity overtakes my anxiety in front of groups.

—Rebecca Campbell, vice president, human resources

The Listener-Friendly Pause

> *The most precious things in speech are the... pauses.*
> —Sir Ralph Richardson

The French composer Claude Debussy, among others, expressed the notion that "music is the space between the notes." Classical pianist Arthur Schnabel said, "The notes I handle no better than many pianists. But the pauses between the notes—ah, that is where the art resides!" In a similar vein, what separates communicators from talkers resides in the micro-pause between sentences, the breath after a spoken paragraph, and the full stop after a big idea.

Much like a beginner guitarist stretching their fingers for the next chord, there may be some initial awkwardness in developing this new habit. But when the practice becomes fluid, your listeners feel nourished by your engagement without knowing how you did it.

Many speakers tend to run their sentences together, often patching transitions with "and" or "so." If given the opportunity to convert their talk into written form, they would no doubt edit with periods and paragraph breaks to make the presentation more "reader friendly." They likely know that filling a page with long sentences and no paragraph breaks would be hard on the eyes and on comprehension, yet when speaking they often offer the verbal equivalent: listener-unfriendly clutter.

Why do we do this? There are plenty of reasons, but at the root of them all, I believe, is our family of origin. As small children, many of us were interrupted and talked over at the slightest pause. Trying to create the new habit of adding that pause back in—even just one second of it—generates anxiety. And taking the verbal equivalent of a paragraph break (perhaps just two to three seconds of silence) or after making a significant point (maybe five or more seconds) can easily conjure up the fear that our listeners will mock us in unison: "Cat got your tongue?!"

When we practice listener-friendly pauses, audience comprehension goes up and we achieve a new level of ease and intelligence on our feet because we have more space and time to think. And the audience has more time to digest our words. As we develop the relational presence "muscle" that supports these golden silences, we also have the opportunity to transform what goes on in them.

A common habit that pops up in the emerging pauses is that of chasing the next thought or line. When the speaker's eyes go to the floor or ceiling, or inward, it signals that they are reaching for what to say next. These moments offer the chance to see what happens when we interrupt this pattern of thinking in isolation. When we put our priority on being with one person's eyes as if we are thinking *together*, dissolving the habit of *dis*connecting to think, we develop the capacity to be *easygoing in the not knowing*, from which naturally arises newfound flow. (The concept of being easygoing in the not knowing is also discussed in chapters 3 and 5.)

Paradoxically, allowing oneself to be at a loss for words in a supportive environment ultimately eliminates the fear of being at a loss for words.

A pause can be such an elegant moment in the choreography of public speaking. It crafts a dance between sound and silence.

—Millie Baker, speaking coach

> **Invitation**—Think ahead to a sensitive conversation you anticipate having in the next few days. In the mirror (aloud or silently), or in turns with your relational presence partner, reflect on your intention to allow more natural pauses than you usually would.

"Hello Silence, My Old Friend"

The right word may be effective, but no word was ever as effective as a rightly timed pause.
—Mark Twain

In an article in *Parabola* Magazine, philosopher William Segal responded to this question:

"Is there a way in which I could practice developing the sensibility and the sensitivity to speak with the kind of freshness which now is missing?" Segal wrote:

> *Most people speak, as the expression goes, from the top of their heads, so the words issue mechanically. A stop, a moment of pause, brings unsuspected energies. There is a change, the quality of energy that's transferred is quite different. But that is not so easy. It's easier to speak from our knowledge, from accumulated experience, from imitation of others.*

Even among professional speakers there is anxiety about stopping regularly for a full breath and conversing at a listener-friendly pace. You may find yourself uncomfortable in front of groups with the natural silences that are common in sensitive one-on-one engagements. Yet natural pauses are precisely what are needed for your listeners to contemplate and absorb your information and your message.

Jack Gescheidt is a forest, climate, and animal rights activist who sought out Speaking Circles in the mid-2000s when he started getting media and TV speaking requests. He was experiencing public speaking anxiety, or as he calls it, "freaking out." Here is what he says about the experience:

Relational presence practice quickly got me past my lifelong abject terror, since grade school, of speaking in front of groups. The fear had been hard-wired from a handful of traumatic speaking experiences—not just in classrooms, but in office conference rooms, and even memorably embarrassing dating experiences. Lee taught me how to slow down, way down.

I was raised in a fast-talking family in a New York City culture that we've seen spoofed in Woody Allen movies. Everyone at the dinner table was trying to talk at once and always competing for attention. That's great training for having a quick, facile mind, but not for serenity and clarity of thought.

Silences didn't come naturally to me, but I've become a far more effective and comfortable speaker since learning to luxuriate in letting my energy come down into a poignant pause after saying something with particular weight. This lets the audience catch up with me and join me in the journey of the range of emotions that flow through me.

I learned, with practice in safe, supportive Circles, the luxury of being on stage in front of an audience, with newfound delight in knowing I wouldn't be interrupted,

Deep relaxed breathing is the difference between anxiety-stricken speakers and relaxed, invigorated, joyous ones.

—Jack Gescheidt

and loving it. Silences didn't come naturally to me, but I retrained my brain and my nervous system to luxuriate in pregnant, even poignant pauses, for audience impact and my own peace of mind—who knew these could be one and the same!

> **Invitation**—In the mirror or in turns with your relational presence partner, reflect on your level of comfort with pauses in your conversations. As you speak, elongate the pauses between sentences and see how that feels.

Your Presence Speaks Louder than Your Words

Never say anything that doesn't improve on silence.
—Richard Yates

When I work with clients in developing talks, the challenge they face is how to be informative without compromising presence. Though they understand that listeners are attracted to presenters who are a pleasure to be with, this quality is missing from many talks because of the perceived pressure to say a lot in a short period of time.

What is important to understand is that presence speaks louder than words. And, with an enhanced presence, your words will have greater impact. So the answer is to practice relational presence as the *only* priority until it becomes second nature for you to fill any room with your inner light. Your train of thought may have to crash and burn a few times until you are able to be easygoing in the not knowing in front of a supportive group or in a Zoom Circle (see Part 3). But with practice, you will get there.

It's clear to an audience when someone is speaking to cover up the discomfort of silence. So the goal is to embrace the pause and let your content emerge from the shared quiet. This is where real power, comfort, and authority originate. You must first learn how to stay out of the way. This is a challenge, of course, since staying out of the way is actually effortless, and it may seem counterintuitive. We tend to believe there's so much work to be done. Right?

Never miss a good chance to shut up.
—Will Rogers

Well, here's the deal. With practice, it becomes second nature to embrace the pause. By doing so, you create an atmosphere in which your audience can access the unadulterated pleasure of your company and relax into the process of hearing and understanding your message. And that is the way to expand your personal and professional influence in the world.

> **Invitation**—In the mirror (aloud or silently), or with your relational presence partner, start your turns by saying, "My presence speaks louder than my words," and see where you go from there.

Be a Provider of Quality Time

We all know what quality time feels like, and there is no such thing as too much of it. Quality time is marked by natural silences, where there is no rush to fill the space with words. Masterful communicators provide wall-to-wall quality time for whomever they are with, whether one person, a small group, or an audience of thousands. They do it with an attitude of

Make sure you have stopped speaking before your audience has stopped listening.
—Dorothy Sarnoff

> *I've begun to realize that you can listen to silence and learn from it. It has a quality and a dimension all its own.*
>
> —Chaim Potok

inclusion and listening eyes that say, "I am here with you and for you." This attitude and these eyes remain steady with one person at a time, when talking and when listening. Providing quality time is their highest priority because they know that doing so brings out the best in others.

Masterful communicators know that providing quality time *saves* time rather than taking time out of their busy day. Quality time saves hours by quickening the meeting of hearts and minds. Leaders who consistently provide quality time build trust and loyalty. When they walk into a room, the space instantly feels warm and inviting. When a speaker provides wall-to-wall quality time from the front of the room, audiences lean in and listen with rapt attention. *What comes across as magnetism is simply the ability to make listeners feel seen and valued as human beings.*

So how does one develop the capacity for this valuable skill? First, you must understand that it's easy and natural. The only "trick" is that to get there you must practice it as your highest priority. Practice being present with one person at a time without having to speak. This might slow you down at first, even stop you in your tracks and raise your anxiety before it lands you in the sweet zone of ease in front of groups. But ultimately, mastering the capacity to be a provider of quality time, anytime and anywhere, improves the quality of your own life and enhances your capacity to live your uniqueness out loud.

Invitation—Reflect on who in your life provides you with quality time, and to whom you provide quality time. In the mirror (aloud or silently), or in turns with your relational presence partner, reflect on what you get and what you give that creates quality time with these people.

8. The Element of Connection

Being relationally present as my priority with audiences has freed me from rigorous process and self-judgment. It also impacts my business since I can show up at peace with no agenda other than to remain naturally connected with my clients.

—Nedra Hines, home stager

Radiate Kind Regard

> *Be kind whenever possible. It is always possible.*
> —Dalai Lama

At the ripe young age of seventy-six it hit me like a ton of feathers that my life had been a journey from niceness (a passive quality) to kindness (an active one). David Levithan said, "Kindness connects to who you are, while niceness connects to how you want to be seen."

I grew up in a family where meanness stomped all over niceness. My mom's parents lived with us when I was ages four to twelve, and the only one in the house with kindness consciousness was Grandma Lena. She was wise enough to keep her mouth shut, so what she passed on to me that saved my soul came through her knowing eyes. Whether sitting by the window and knitting, which she did much of the day, or clanking through the house on crutches and a wooden leg, whenever we crossed paths she never failed to convey a potent micro-dose of loving kindness through her eyes. By her letting me know I was okay, a door to self-kindness cracked open within me.

It lately occurred to me that Grandma Lena likely knew exactly what she was doing as she systematically administered the healing power of kindness to the chubby, lonely, preternaturally self-conscious misfit under her roof. Without those thousands of silent interventions, I doubt I would have had the inner resources to recover somewhat intact from my childhood. Ultimately, those moments allowed me to find my life work treating thousands of others to generous doses of kind regard.

I've opened Speaking Circles retreats by asking participants to close their eyes and remember someone who really saw them and heard them early in life. I ask them to imagine gazing softly into the eyes of that person and to breathe in the feeling of being fully seen and accepted. Then I suggest that they listen to others in the session through the eyes of that person, and I let them know that I am listening to them through Grandma Lena's eyes.

The many therapists, coaches, and other practitioners who've come through Speaking Circles are aware of the value of listening with kind regard in their own work, as are businesspeople wise enough to know that this kind of listening to clients, customers, and colleagues is a key to success. And aren't we all aware that listening to friends and loved ones from a position of kindness whenever possible works wonders?

Kindness is more important than wisdom, and the recognition of this is the beginning of wisdom.

—Theodore Isaac Rubin

> **Invitation**—Do my memories of Grandma Lena inspire you to think of someone who saw you (or currently sees you) that way? Gaze at yourself in the mirror through that person's kind eyes, or with your relational presence partner take turns seeing the other through those eyes, and reflect on this question: Who in your life these days gets that kind of seeing and listening from *you*? And to whom would you like to intentionally provide this lifeline?

The Healing Energy of Natural Connection

At one of my Speaking Circles, seven experienced participants allowed their content to emerge and flow at its own pace without a plan, creating an elegant smorgasbord of soulful humanity. Then the newcomer in the room started his turn by clasping his chest and expressing the frustration of having "all this energy inside that I don't know how to get out." After he spoke another sentence in exasperation and not into the eyes of any listener, I invited him to stay with one person at a time. Fortunately, he was coachable, and by the end of the turn, he too had settled into effortless flow. When I asked how the experience was for him, he indicated that he felt fully expressed, his energy unstuck.

That's when it hit home for me how the human connection we foster in relational presence practice comes with powerful healing energy. By simply inviting the person up front to breathe and allow the energy of human connection to run its natural course, the connection reveals itself. This requires no doing, just being.

A positive outcome of this practice is finding ourselves naturally bringing this effortless energy of connection into everyday life. Whether I'm having a difficult conversation or a loving moment, when I remember to breathe and allow the natural energy of connection to flow, things take a turn for the better. I see now that true healers in any modality simply allow the natural human connection to thrive in their presence.

> *I define connection as the energy that exists between people when they feel seen, heard, and valued; when they can give and receive without judgment.*
> —Brené Brown

Shedding one's armor in front of audiences allows the kind of connection that many people spend a lifetime searching for.
—Julia Rebecca Miron, mindfulness teacher

> **Invitation**—Softly gaze into the mirror and explore what it's like to allow healing energy to run between you and your reflection for several easy breaths. Or do this together with your relational presence partner.

Realize the Paradox of Time

> How did it get so late so soon?
> It's night before it's afternoon.
> December is here before it's June.
> My goodness how the time has flewn.
> How did it get so late so soon?
> —Dr. Seuss

Dr. Jacob Needleman, in an interview discussing his book *Time and the Soul* (1997), said:

> *There have been countless ingenious technological innovations the past 200 years, in the last 50 years especially, all designed to save us time. Remarkable inventions. Somehow, the result has been that nobody has any time left. Why? What is that all about?*

As Needleman pointed out, this is the paradox of time in our modern age; that the urgent quickening drumbeat of imposed artificial external time has been obliterating our natural inner quality of eternal timelessness, where the truth of who we really are resides. Decades of relational presence practice with groups has gotten me to a place where I effortlessly facilitate a luxurious sense of timelessness that brings listeners in any room into their essential knowing. But when I am not in front of a group, I am often at the mercy of that "urgent drumbeat of imposed external time" that is our modern plague.

My challenge is to translate my ease with groups to my time alone. With groups I am *easygoing in the not knowing* by being with one person at a time as if they were the only person in the world. I don't make an effort to connect (which would be coming from a sense of separateness) but rather gently *allow* the natural connection between us to arise. The energy of this connection with one person draws the entire group along and creates a field of clarity that includes everyone in the room. When you are in relational presence with an audience, the urgent drumbeat of external time fades off into the past.

So how can I do this alone with myself in the middle of a hectic workday when I really need respite? I can tap into a state of relational presence between the two parts of myself: the busy external timekeeper, and the timeless inner essence. Through the lens of the timeless one I can see the busy one as trying to do his best to take care of business. And through the lens of the busy one I can see the timeless one creating space for true fulfillment. And when I am able to do this for myself, as with a group, I can almost hear that urgent drumbeat fade away.

> **Invitation**—In the mirror (aloud or silently), or in turns with your partner, reflect on the impact in your life of "the urgent drumbeat of external time."

Public Speaking as a Spiritual Path

Speaking to a group evokes unease because the confrontation throws many into existential fragility. This predictable response provides a golden opportunity to *stop the world*, take a breath, and intentionally invite our oneness with humanity into the mix.

Conventional physics had no place for non-material concepts, but quantum physics now supports the core spiritual value of the oneness of humanity as a scientific reality.

Sharing from a sense of oneness is where authentic connection begins for a speaker. After decades of abject public speaking anxiety, I found a way to approach an audience from a sense of oneness, and I devised a protocol that seamlessly guides others to do the same.

You see, if you *try* to bring a sense of oneness into a room through technique or effort, it doesn't get you there because you are coming from a mindset of separateness. Rather, the core practice of relational presence—being with one person at a time and seeing them so they feel seen—naturally leads to a group *experience* of oneness. Next time you are feeling a strong connection with a speaker, notice if you are also feeling connected with the others in the audience.

I was taught as a child that God is all around me and to never feel insufficient. Decades later, Speaking Circles helped my talks all the more embody that truth.
—Carol Soucek King, MFA, PhD

Invitation—In the mirror (aloud or silently), or in turns with your relational presence partner, reflect on the notion of the oneness of humanity, even including people you may not feel good about.

> *Always treat your employees exactly as you want them to treat your best customers.*
>
> —Stephen Covey

Save Time by Taking Time to Allow Connection

Max was an in-house trainer for a Fortune 500 retail clothing chain. It was his job to orient new clerks and cashiers to the customer service culture and procedures of the company. At trainings, he'd stand in front of the group of predominantly young employees, his heart pounding, and work hard to take command. He was often distressed by what he saw as disinterest and disrespect, which caused him to ratchet up his energy and power through the resistance. He eventually got his points across, but he felt totally drained at the end of every day. He didn't feel he was long for the job.

What Max learned through relational presence practice reminded him of what his high school football coach had worked with him on years before. A third-string quarterback, Max remembered the coach stressing that the difference between a good QB and a great one has little to do with arm strength or accuracy. Greatness shows up in how he sees the whole field, in the moment before he throws a pass—or chooses *not* to throw a pass.

With snarling 250-pounders bearing down on him, a quarterback often has less than a second to make that decision. The coach told him that in that moment of truth, the great quarterbacks "stop time," get quiet, breathe, and see everything all at once with no pressure to make anything happen. The sports vernacular is that "they let the game come to them." As a result, the action a quarterback takes is less a decision than a natural flow of events that he becomes part of.

Max realized that standing in front of a group of resistant trainees was bringing out exactly the same performance pressure to make something happen he'd faced as a young quarterback. But relational presence practice gave him copious opportunities and support to slow down that moment, see it in stop-action, recognize internally what assumptions and unexamined reactions were in the way of full engagement with his groups, and replace those habits with new ones.

Now when Max stands up in front of a new group his heart still pounds, but instead of rushing into the information, he takes a full breath of silence and regards his audience with respect. Instead of grabbing command of the group, he lets them come to him. He finds a receptive face and starts by conversationally relating a vignette from his life when he was a new and stressed-out clerk. The rest of the training flows from there. Here's what Max reported to me:

> *I never have to raise my voice anymore. When someone asks a challenging question, instead of reacting defensively like before, I stop, take a breath, relax, and see the whole field. The answer comes naturally and clearly. Sometimes I ask someone else in the group if they would like to respond, and when they do, they are usually on the money!*
>
> *The extra time these silences take might add up to a minute every hour, tops. But they set a tone of mutual respect and pleasurable learning that allows at least fifteen more minutes of important information to*

be transmitted and digested than when I used to "take command." I love my work now.

> **Invitation**—Reflect on how you react when someone challenges your opinion or belief or asks you a question that makes you feel defensive. In the mirror (aloud or silently), or in turns with your relational presence partner, reflect on this and imagine what it would be like next time this happens to take a full breath before responding (or choosing not to respond).

PART 2

On Giving a Talk

9.

Developing Talk Content

Embracing your personal story is one of the most powerful things you will ever do. Having the courage to share it—even the messy, imperfect parts—can transform you and the people around you.

—Katherine Kennedy, storytelling coach and author of *Speaking to What Matters*

From Katherine Kennedy's Book: *Speaking to What Matters*

One day, when I was a student in high school, I was rushing from a meeting to a class when the school counselor intercepted me and asked me into his office. He said, "Katherine, I see you working so hard on behalf of everyone. I can often hear your laugh in the hallway. But sometimes I look at you and wonder if you are okay. Are you okay?"

Inside I panicked. *How did he know? Who else could tell?* Then I cried and cried and couldn't speak. But if those tears could talk, they would have said, *I'm alone. I'm miserable, and I'm so tired of pretending everything is okay.*

That was a turning point in my life, the stark realization that I was living behind a mask and in so much fear I couldn't share the truth of the isolation and depression inside. I eventually found a career path that entailed learning how to help young people express themselves through sharing their story. In the process of helping others, I learned how to access the truth of my own story and to step into a braver, more authentic version of myself.

Suggested Structure of an Effective Talk

So far in this book, the emphasis has been on what might be called "the inner game of public speaking," featuring the mastery of relational presence. The next step is to understand how to structure a talk to allow for the implementation of relational presence. There are several ways to structure an effective talk. In this chapter, we will discuss one way to do that.

Your Opening: Start with a Scene from Your Life
Co-authored with Doreen Downing

If you are developing a talk to spread the word about a service, practice, product, or cause, we suggest you begin with a brief turning point story. Katherine Kennedy's story above is a perfect example. The idea is to give your audience a strong sense of where you are coming from and why you do what you do. Marketing guru Simon Sinek said, "People don't buy what you do, they buy why you do it." (Search online for his TED Talk, "How great leaders inspire action.")

Before you tell your story, you want to take at least one full breath while looking around the audience. (See Take Your All-Important Opening Breath, page 148.) And instead of opening with a nicety or an attention-grabbing statement, start with one sentence that paints a scene that your audience can picture as they would, say, the opening scene in a movie about your life. This sentence will lead into your turning point story, which shouldn't take more than two minutes to tell. It may be an episode within the larger story that will show up in the body of the talk. This opening vignette should culminate in a realization or paradigm shift that inspired your life's work going forward, a significant aspect of which you are about to share with your listeners.

Stories constitute the single most powerful weapon in a leader's arsenal.
—Howard Gardner

A simply told life moment becomes a universally shared experience for an audience. We each have hundreds of such life moments archived in our psyche, but they are often below the level of consciousness, latent. When we allow relaxed time to recall them, more come into consciousness, sometimes in a flood of memories. Keeping a Life Moments journal can be helpful.

So, back to your first sentence. This sentence wants to be delivered with just enough information to allow your listeners to visualize the scene and join you in the moment. Your opening sentence is best spoken conversationally into the eyes of a listener who is paying attention. Concise and clear, it conveys a time, a place, and a universally understood situation. A good opening sentence evokes a clear mental picture that transports a group to that moment and draws them in to hear the rest of the story.

At a networking meeting I attended some forty years ago, a CPA opened his ten-minute talk with this sentence: "When I was a boy, every night my parents would fight bitterly in the next room, and the walls were paper thin." Can you see the clear scene he painted? He continued:

> *I couldn't sleep so I counted sheep with numbers on their backs. The numbers sometimes went into the thousands before I'd be able to fall asleep. This nightly practice made me relaxed around big numbers, and I eventually became an accountant. Now it gives me great pleasure to relax you around your numbers.*

I immediately knew that I wanted to work with this man, and he became my accountant for ten years. When he moved into portfolio management, he continued to get my business. All because of a thirty-second personal story.

> **Invitation**—Write down some turning point life moments you recall. You might start a Life Stories or Life Moments journal to collect such stories going forward. As this chapter continues, these stories will come into play.

The Rest of Your Opening

After you deliver your opening sentence, you want to take a full breath while the audience registers the scene and gathers their attention to hear more. You use this breath yourself as well, to go back in time to feel into the moment. As mentioned above, the rest of your opening story needs to be concise, perhaps just one or two minutes, because at this point too much information will be difficult to digest for many listeners. Be clear and conversational, with no misdirection, drama, or embellishment. Be real about what happened but avoid going on any detours. You want to let your listeners have their own experience, not transfix them with yours.

Here's an opening sentence from my training partner, Doreen Downing: "When I was six years old my dad left home forever without explanation, and my mom never talked about it." (Get the clear picture?) After a full breath she goes

Speakers who talk about what life has taught them never fail to keep the attention of their listeners.

—Dale Carnegie

on to tell how this miserable reality led her to a decades-long career as a psychologist, in which she masterfully decodes toxic secrets in family systems.

I worked with a financial consultant who opened this way: "When I was a child, every few months we would pack all our belongings in the car and my father would drive us to another town to stay one step ahead of the bill collector." (Again, a clear picture.) After a full breath, he told how he vowed to himself that he would never do anything like that when he had a family; and to make sure, he studied the world of finance and found a career there.

Here's an example of how you can take just about anything currently happening in your life and see it as a turning point story. At one of our Speaking Circles facilitator trainings, the group was sitting around the table for Saturday dinner—a raucous occasion marked by spontaneous singing and stories—when one of our participants looked pained. Someone asked if she was okay. The room came to a hush as this person broke into tears and told us how she was seeing everyone else as great speakers and herself as pathetic. After we let her words and emotions land and have space, I asked if she'd be willing to tell this story as a life moment. She nodded yes, took a deep breath, and started: "Two minutes ago I was sitting at this table feeling like a failure." Taking in our rapt listening, she took a few long, deep breaths, and eloquently connected this experience with patterns in her past. She realized the truth of the moment, remembered who she was, and spun out a teaching that we could each apply to our own self-esteem challenges.

> **Invitation**—Take one or more of your turning point stories and write about how it impacted your life. What did you learn? What was the meaning and message of what happened?

What to Do After You Tell Your Story
Co-authored with Doreen Downing

So you have told your opening story. Now what? Here's a format that we find very effective.

> **What you learned.** When the action in the story ends, take a full breath and talk about what you came away with or learned in that experience. Focus on what in the experience informed and inspired your life path and body of work. What about it brings you here today to talk about [your topic]?
>
> **Your promise.** What's in it for your audience? In one sentence, make the strongest promise that you expect to deliver. In marketing, this is known as "benefits, not features." Then take a full breath.
>
> **Their agreement.** Collect their agreement that they are in the right room and are willing to make the journey with you. You may ask something like "Are you ready?" or "Would this be helpful?" Remember to be with one person at a time in relational presence. At this point you can expect a sea of faces nodding "Yes, yes, we are with you!" Notice this.

Your opening has a finite ending to separate it from the body of your talk. You have provided crystal clarity on who you are, why you are here, what you will do, and what's in it for them, which are the four elements they need to know to give you their undivided listening. And you have obtained their agreement that they are eager to hear what you have to say.

This entire opening should be no more than five minutes. In fact, it is actually a closing (as in "closing" a sale), since the intention is to close your listeners on being with you body, mind, and soul. This provides the ground into which your information and message can now flow to them.

The Body of Your Talk

After your opening, we see the body of an effective talk as having three sections and a closing:

1. Awareness of the Problem/Pain/Suffering you are addressing.

2. The transformational Point of View/ New Thinking/New Paradigm you are offering.

3. Action Steps you will suggest.

1. **Awareness of the Problem.** Here you would provide a discussion of the problem you are here to help solve, the associated suffering you are here to alleviate. There might be statistics, examples, relevant aspects of your own story. You might talk about things you and others have tried that didn't solve it. In this section you would

make no mention of how you will be approaching and solving these aspects of the problem.

2. **New Point of View.** We have often found that the real problem is that we have been misperceiving and tackling the problem from the wrong end. For example, when I do a presentation about how to heal public speaking anxiety, I make clear that the problem is not a block in *speaking*, which is a common way of looking at it, but a block in receiving the available *listening*. Most authorities in all fields have gotten to a point where conventional wisdom gets turned on its head. Your *aha!* here is the turning point of your talk.

3. **Action Steps.** Here is where you lay out your program to solve the problem, the action steps you recommend to your audience, which at this point they are eager to hear. There's a reason why you wait until now to do so. It is common for speakers to start solving the problem in question way too early in a talk. You see, solutions doled out before an audience can identify with the depth of suffering we are dealing with, and before entertaining a new way to think about what the real problem is, often fall on deaf ears. By fully engaging the audience before serving up the main course, you have whetted their appetite for your solutions.

Your Closing. After at least one full breath, you may have a climactic update of your opening story that brings home your message, though that's not necessary. In any case, we hold that your last words should be unscripted appreciation for your audience, with you looking forward to working with them again. Some speakers script a rousing, inspirational closing designed to garner a standing ovation, but we see the end of a talk as an *opening* to long-term business relationships with audience members. Heartfelt words as you lovingly look around the room is what is called for at this point.

> **Invitation**—Take one or more of your life stories and write about how the event significantly changed your thinking. In addition to writing, you might practice relational presence in the mirror (aloud or silently), or with a partner, either before sitting down to write, or as a summary after you have jotted down a first draft.

Embracing Your Life Story

"Every now and again I open my mouth and fire comes out.
—Katherine Kennedy

In helping people tell their story, storytelling coach Katherine Kennedy emphasizes the importance of getting crystal clear on the core challenge the storyteller faced in their life and the choices they made over time to become a truer version of the person they are meant to be. She says:

> *The beautiful thing about the "choice" part of the journey is that as you recount the choices you've made over time, you get to learn your values and who you're becoming.*

And the "change" part is beautiful because you get to see what you've learned about yourself and what aspect of wisdom you can pass on to others. We never tire of hearing about other people's journeys and finding the hero and the heroine in each of us.

The author of her own life story, *Speaking to What Matters* (2023), Kennedy says that in developing a talk in which to share one's story, a common mistake is to prematurely craft a script. She encourages you instead to tell your story over and over again into good listening, whether to friends, colleagues, or a coach. She advises her clients to come at the story in different ways, to go deeper, and to reflect. She asks questions that invite them to keep digging. She suggests they attend Speaking Circles, as she does, to share aspects of their story and experience the transformative power of sharing what's inside in a safe, welcoming environment. Kennedy says:

This process of learning how to reply to the age-old request "Tell me about yourself" is universal. With each client, with every single interaction, I discover again and again that our ability to describe who we are, what we do, and why we do it is rooted in our story. In it, we discover our values and defining moments. We discover ourselves.

Invitation—See if you can identify a major life challenge that your stories point to, and write about it.

Tap into Your Rage to Contribute

> *Freedom is what you do with what's been done to you.*
> —Attributed to Jean-Paul Sartre

True leaders heed the call to live out loud through events in their lives that demand participation from a deeply emotional place. For example, since contracting Parkinson's, the actor Michael J. Fox's advocacy for those with the disease became his life's work. Most emotional storylines, however, are less obvious. Many of us were born into adverse circumstances or suffered hardships in life. At the same time, each of us entered the world with an inherent capacity for creative problem-solving. Those who are able to survive and thrive often become passionate about lending a hand to others who still suffer.

Years, or even decades, of experience transcending your greatest challenges has given you an evolving mastery. Embrace it! Your unique expertise may or may not yet have a name, but it is a potency within that cries out for full-throated voice. You may not yet be aware of it consciously, but I assure you that if you are reading this book you are on the path to expressing your gift in a way that attracts the people for whom you can make a difference.

> *Although the world is full of suffering, it is also full of the overcoming of it.*
> —Helen Keller

I have come to realize that I have a *rage* to contribute. As elucidated earlier in this book, my primary emotional storyline is that as a child I was neither seen nor heard. My natural expression was squelched and remained underground for forty-five years. Then I found a way out that allowed me to become a transformational agent for others whose self-consciousness and performance anxiety were stifling their voice and compromising their gifts. My rage to contribute alchemically transmuted into Speaking Circles, the concept of relational presence, and whatever else is yet to come. As I put this book together at age eighty, *the fire in me rages on*. Exploring the emotional storyline that informs your unique gifts in the world will organically lead to stories that invite connection with listeners.

A Speaking Circles participant was inspired by my writings to talk about her emotional storyline at the next session. Later she emailed:

> *I had never before spoken about my life into this kind of spacious listening. The experience gave me clarity about severe obstacles that have taken decades to overcome. I left with a clear sense of where I want to put my life energy going forward.*

The only way to speak from the bottom of your heart is to be absolutely real with your audience. Nothing less works for me.
—Brandy Jones, financial consultant

Invitation—Can you identify a desire within to contribute to making this a better world? Reflect on that in the mirror (aloud or silently), or in turns with your relational presence partner.

On Being a Change Agent

Change agents are inspired to make a difference in the world by addressing, in the context of their field, the primary cause of psychic suffering among humans, which is the illusion of separateness—from self and from humanity. To be human is to live in the apparent duality of our immortal divine essence on the one hand, and our problem-solving mind and mortal body on the other.

Every great vision begins with a heavy burden in the heart of a visionary. Any vision that never begins with a burden is a mere fantasy and will not carry any fire that's capable of driving a change agent or the revivalist.

—Benjamin Suulola

As an executive coach who specializes in guiding CEOs through crucial transitions, David Lesser deals with this duality daily. His task is to meet leaders where they are. For example, when they see their situation as a problem to be fixed, he invites them into a more complete experience of who they are and what is really going on for them. In our conversation, Lesser pinpointed his challenge working with CEOs hell-bent on problem-solving when he knows that the deeper issue is related to their separation from self. His work requires that he engage with them on the level of problem-solving, which is also a strength of his, while holding a potent space for the underlying truth to breathe through.

While such "evolutionary edge walking," as Lesser calls it, can be an excruciating experience at times, it points to the place within that change agents are called to heal. Perhaps you are among the many change-agents-in-training who are not yet clear about the specific message they are meant to share in the world, or perhaps not sure about the identity of their audience. Getting spacious listening (not of the problem-solving variety), one-on-one or with a supportive group, will help uncover the pearls of essential knowing within.

> **Invitation**—Are you a change agent? If you often feel an inner calling to make a difference in the world, you likely are. In the mirror (aloud or silently), or in turns with your relational presence partner, reflect on yourself as a change agent.

Dare Greatly

If you haven't viewed Brené Brown's marvelous 2010 TEDx talk "The Power of Vulnerability," please do. It is a model of what relational presence on a big stage looks like. In her Netflix special of 2019, Brown talks about the spiral of shame she experienced after that talk upon reading social media comments that included body shaming. Recovery came when she happened on this famous quote from a 1910 speech given by Theodore Roosevelt:

It's easy to count other people's mistakes. Make your own if you can.
—Ljupka Cvetanova

> *It is not the critic who counts; not the man who points out how the strong man stumbles, or where the doer of deeds could have done them better. The credit belongs to the man who is actually in the arena, whose face is marred by dust and sweat and blood; who strives valiantly; who errs, who comes short again and again, because there is no effort without error and shortcoming; but who does actually strive to do the deeds; who knows the great enthusiasms, the great devotions; who spends himself in a worthy cause; who at the best knows in the end the triumph of high achievement, and who at the worst, if he fails, at least fails while daring greatly. . . .*

The more vulnerable I reveal myself to be, the greater my chance to empower others.
—Phil Blagg, firefighter

In Brown's book *Daring Greatly: How the Courage to Be Vulnerable Transforms the Way We Live, Love, Parent, and Lead* (2015), she expands on her debt to Teddy Roosevelt and encourages her readers to put themselves out there, that the fear of judgment and criticism should not stop them. It is my experience that Speaking Circles are useful for those who are called to show up in the arena rather than just commenting from the bleachers.

> **Invitation**—If you were to "dare greatly" to do something, how would that daring show up in the world? Reflect on this in the mirror (aloud or silently), or in turns with your relational presence partner.

Live Your Life Purpose Out Loud

Effective communication is 20% what you know and 80% how you feel about what you know.
—Jim Rohn

Although Speaking Circles are known for dissolving public speaking anxiety and supporting authenticity with groups, they also provide access to clearer expression of one's purpose in life. This hit home when my business coach, Audrey Seymour, forwarded an article that made my heart leap: "Soul Meets Purpose: Are your client's goals driven by ego or soul?" by executive coach Tim Kelley. (You can find this by searching online for "Tim Kelley Choice Article.")

Kelley suggests that our life purpose is set by soul and is invisible to our everyday mind. True purpose cannot be brainstormed, problem-solved, nor goal oriented. Goals, he writes, are "set by ego, with varying degrees of influence from the soul. A goal that serves my client is one that is consistent with his or her purpose, and the soul is the keeper of the purpose, not the ego." By this view, if you are not clear about your essential life purpose, goals are but heady guesses.

So how can we think about our true purpose and talk about it from a soulful place that is attuned to the available listening? In this regard, I know from personal experience that the coaches in Tim Kelley's True Purpose Institute do masterful work one-on-one. And through Speaking Circles I've found that with groups, relational presence naturally calms the ego and facilitates soul-to-soul transmission.

Speaking Circles participants share the higher purpose of simply being ourselves out loud. Now I see that *content* that arises into the listening sometimes affords clues to the soul transmission of *specific* purpose. Creating safe spaces for others to access, express, and live their life purpose out loud is *my* life purpose. Read the next essay to see where that has taken me.

> **Invitation**—Are you curious about your life purpose? Reflect on that in the mirror (aloud or silently), or in turns with your relational presence partner.

Life Purpose Clarity Sessions

I learned from Tim Kelley, mentioned in the previous section, that goals are often heady guesses set by ego, while one's essential purpose in life is set by soul. This led me to create and refine a 30-minute Life Purpose Clarity session (in-person or via Zoom) designed to work wonders for anyone curious about their life purpose. I will share here how I do this so you

Stop searching so hard for what you think are the "right" answers and listen to what you already know to help guide you.
—Skylar Sustin

might recreate it with a good listener in your life who is also curious about their life purpose.

In these sessions, we bypass problem-solving mode in favor of soulful sharing, which is where life purpose shines through. As coach/facilitator, my work is to evoke a soulful memory that leads to an epiphany that relates to a significant aspect of your life purpose that would be useful to know. A story that arises into good listening can provide clues to an unexpected aspect of one's true purpose. This almost always leads to valuable insights and practical ideas.

There are many possible ways to immediately engage the soul. Here is what has worked for me that will hopefully inspire your own approach. My favorite is that in advance of the session I ask for a song that has meaning in the person's life. I've found that most people have a song like this, perhaps a few, though they may have to think about it a little.

Soon after the start of the session, I soulfully sing a few lines from the song and invite the person to join me. Usually they do. After taking a breath together, I ask, "So . . . where does this song live in you now?" From here our dialogue invariably lands them in a significant story, perhaps a turning point in their life that relates to their life purpose. Further discussion and *ahas!* ensue, along with a practical step or two toward living out that purpose.

I worked with a psychologist and mother of two young girls. She had an interest in speaking to groups about parenting, but public speaking anxiety was holding her back. To start our session, we sang together a few lines of a song that was meaningful to her—the Beatles' *Here Comes the Sun*. When I asked where the song lives in her, she said, "Right here in my belly. It's like I'm giving birth to the sun, and the light is going up to my throat and I'm excited about what wants to come out."

She immediately saw that what wants to come out is her message to parents, which includes: "Observe how you are talking to yourself because that's exactly how you are talking to and disciplining your children. And how you talk to your children becomes *their* inner voice." She was thrilled to discover this and told me: "My desire to deliver that message to parents is more powerful than my fear of speaking!" As a result, she joined a public speaker mastermind group to develop and practice her talk.

I conducted another session with an executive coach who, after twenty-two years, strongly sensed "something new" was next and wanted clarity around what it might be. I asked for a song, and she said with a big smile, "I have a *movie* that has a lot of meaning to me." She then spoke passionately for ten minutes about *Harold and Maude*, a fifty-year-old cult classic. Later she wrote:

> *Our session was a launching pad for me to be curious about why I picked this movie. What is it about these characters that moves me? How do these characters live inside me? What might they tell me? The answers allowed me to claim something important for this next chapter of my life. They pointed me to an aspect of myself that needed witnessing and integration. There is*

something I need to see in myself in order to live my purpose! Our session gave me a doorway to experience more courage and initiative to go where my heart wants to lead me. While I'm not yet clear on my purpose, I am clearer on what it will feel like.

Since these early sessions, I've found a range of possibilities that work for others in quickly bringing soul into the conversation, such as "What book has been meaningful in your life?" and "What person made (or is making) a difference in your life?"

> **Invitation**—Toward clarifying your life's purpose, think of some songs, books, or people that have meaning in your life. If you are willing, do a version of the Life Purpose Clarity process above by singing some lines from a song, feeling into where that song lives in you now, and writing down what life story it leads to and what that might inform you about your life's purpose. Or try the process with your relational presence partner.

Befriend Your Inner Genius

The genius of each of us is to be uniquely ourselves.
—Michael Meade

Lately I've been thinking about the nature of "genius." I'm particularly attracted to the kind of genius that is hard-earned. In his book, *Outliers: The Story of Success* (2008), Malcolm Gladwell writes about his rule of thumb that 10,000 hours of practice is necessary to master anything worth mastering.

Many of us start our first 10,000-hour mastery at a young age as we begin to devise, refine, and ultimately apply strategies to overcome our own neuro/chemical/biological birth diversities or early childhood trauma—or a complex cocktail of both. Equipped with this practice, many of us ultimately enter professions devoted to helping others with similar challenges. As discussed in the chapter on how to structure an effective talk, my friend and training partner Doreen Downing can trace the roots of her forty-year career in the field of psychology to her dad deserting the family without explanation when she was six.

Others find ingenious ways to deal with seemingly impossible challenges, as I did in solving public speaking anxiety after decades of stage terror. Having been born somewhere on the neurodiversity spectrum and having played the role of family problem child, it makes sense that I went on to devise a safe place for myself and others to discover, explore, and share our latent gifts in a warm, receptive listening environment.

In the overview of his audio course series titled The Soul of Genius, storyteller and mythologist Michael Meade writes:

The original idea of genius refers to the inborn spirit and natural gifts of each person. In that sense, everyone has a genius nature and something essential to give to the world. There may be no greater time for people to awaken to the inner spark of genius than the troubling times in which we live.

Psychologist Gay Hendricks, author of *The Zone of Genius*, said in a Franklin-Covey podcast:

> *I don't think of "genius" as wild and crazy as a lot of people think it is. I'm very much interested in a practical approach to genius where people find out what their unique abilities are and then express those in their family, in their friendships, and in their work life so that everybody gets to participate in everybody else's genius.*

In his book *Callings: Finding and Following an Authentic Life* (1997), author and speaker Gregg Levoy points out that Winston Churchill, who became an eloquent orator, was dyslexic and stuttered as a child. Levoy suggests:

> *Instead of seeing children who stutter or cower or are excruciatingly shy as having developmental problems, consider that they may have some great thing inside them, that their symptoms are protecting a gift.*

> **Invitation**—Are you up for befriending your inner genius? In the mirror (aloud or silently), or in turns with your relational presence partner, reflect on what your genius might be.

Speak from Your Essential Knowing
Co-authored with Doreen Downing

When you develop a natural capacity to flow your content through relational presence, you can inspire others to real change and right action. You come into right relationship with your audience by starting with the focus on them. Rather than "Let me tell you about . . . ," you want to extend an invitation: "Come with me on a journey to the heart of our shared humanness."

When you establish this relationship through a relevant opening story, your listeners breathe easy and are receptive to the information. Ultimately, your message wants to come from what we are calling your *essential knowing*. In devising talks from their body of knowledge, many speakers often leave out the raw human struggle of how they came into what they know now at the core of their being. Or in using personal stories to make teaching points they too often fall into the habit of reusing the same "signature story." Aspiring speakers often emulate this conventional standard by embellishing, polishing, and rehearsing turning point stories from their lives, to be told over and over again the same way.

This approach may create energetic presentations, but to the extent that speakers hide behind the craft of it, it distances them from the hearts and souls of their audiences. A talk thriving with life and electricity derives its content from the *essential knowing*, the raw wisdom the speaker earned working with inner and outside challenges. That wisdom wants to now be expressed authentically in the connected moment, rather than performed from a script.

What makes a speaker accessible and irresistible to an audience is a willingness to share in raw form some aspect of what it took to get here. Listeners recognize truth when it is shared, and they can find the place within themselves

Even though there are no ways of knowing for sure, there are ways of knowing for pretty sure.
—Lemony Snicket

that resonates with the speaker's truth. Weaving strands of essential knowing into a talk is an organic process that can evolve through the intelligent listening of a supportive group. But a listening partner with whom to share stories and *aha!* moments (as well as setbacks) on our wisdom journey is also an invaluable resource.

Quality listening from shared stillness allows content threads to arise at their own pace. Keeping a story journal is useful. Life moments that emerge, some perhaps long forgotten, can weave strands of meaning and message into your talks. Not all of these moments lead to the kind of signature stories common among professional speakers. Rather, they are the earthy, conversational bite-size vignettes that make a talk vibrate with humanity.

> **Invitation**—Reflect on the raw wisdom you have earned working with inner and outside challenges. In the mirror (aloud or silently), or in turns with your relational presence partner, reflect on this.

Choose Presence

Anxiety is the dizziness of freedom.
—Søren Kierkegaard

I worked with a young woman to develop a talk, and what a captivating opening story she had! At sixteen, she and her mom made a death-defying escape from occupied Czechoslovakia. They emigrated to the United States, where the girl survived a suicide attempt after a boy broke her heart. She went on to go to school to become a lawyer but soon felt suffocated in that profession before breaking free to find fulfillment as a life coach.

Exciting, yes. But what's the thread and the point? Here's what we worked out: She fought for physical and political freedom. She fought for psychological and financial freedom. She fought for creative and vocational freedom. Now she is free free free and speaking to American audiences, who were born into freedom but often feel imprisoned in our ruts.

So, what is the secret to achieving the holy grail of freedom that so many never do achieve? Her conclusion . . . : You have to consciously *choose freedom*. Over and over again. Or you can't have it. That's her transformational message, and she goes on to discuss exactly how one might make that choice in every moment of truth that arises. Compelling, yes?

I have come to realize that *choosing presence* is a similar dynamic. In front of a group, it's a choice to keep making until it becomes a habit such that *presence chooses you* and the struggle to fully engage with groups is over. The only way I know to choose presence at any moment is to find a listener to be with and breathe with.

> **Invitation**—Reflect on what it would mean for you to "choose presence" over and over again as your priority in front of groups. In the mirror (aloud or silently), or in turns with your relational presence partner, reflect on this.

Find a Hidden Strength

> *We don't even know how strong we are until we are forced to bring that hidden strength forward.*
> —Isabel Allende

I was part of the San Francisco comedy scene in the mid-1970s and was in the room when Robin Williams got up for the first time at an open mic. He got no laughs. Williams had been a classically trained actor at the Juilliard School, where an actor did not break the fourth wall between themself and the audience. He did his open mic piece as theater, which does not work in a stand-up comedy setting.

A quick learner, the next time up he flowed energetically through that fourth wall into the hearts and souls of his audience and got big laughs with the same material. He was on his way! As we came to see, his in-the-moment, audience-grabbing way of comedy turned out to be his major strength, a strength he didn't know he had as a comic until he needed to use it.

Those who regularly attend Speaking Circles often find hidden strengths in the course of their turns. For example:

- A mother of two children, ages four and seven, thought she had a weakness around controlling her anxiety when the kids demanded more attention than she could give. But since practicing relational presence, when one child speaks out or acts up now, she stops what she's doing, gently drops to their level, takes a breath, and hears them out with a soft, steady gaze of kind regard. When they feel seen, they calm down. Taking that extra time *saves* a lot of time, and aggravation. She sees that "dealing with demanding children" is now a strength she'd like to teach other parents.

- A businessman became self-conscious and flustered at meetings when put on the spot with questions and challenges. Through relational presence practice, he discovered that when asked a sensitive question or challenged in any way, instead of pressuring himself to respond quickly, all he need do is take a relaxed full breath. The words that come to him after that breath arise naturally from his gut, and others are now seeing him as a leader.

- A computer software salesman attended a weekend Speaking Circles retreat out of concern that he was losing credibility with business groups because his face turned beet red when he spoke. In his first turns at the workshop, he did indeed blush, but only when he expressed embarrassment about it did his face turn a deeper shade of red. When invited to take his time, just breathe and not try to fix anything, the blush didn't escalate and just took on the look of passion for what he was talking about. He was able to see this in the videos of his turns, and he came out of the workshop realizing that the visibility of his passion would be a strength of his going forward.

In Speaking Circles I first discovered that humor arises naturally from just being myself instead of trying to be funny.
—Matt Weinstein, founder and emperor of Playfair, Inc.

Invitation—Think of something you were really good at in your life, but haven't done much of in several years. In the mirror (aloud or silently), or in turns with your relational presence partner, reflect on what that was and how it might be a clue to a hidden strength that would be useful to develop.

Be Clutter-Free in Your Speaking

If it takes a lot of words to say what you have in mind, give it more thought.

—Dennis Roth

I was preparing to present at a conference of the National Association of Professional Organizers (NAPO) on how to use speaking opportunities to both educate the public on what professional organizers do and to promote their business. I would be guiding these decluttering masters in speaking to potential clients in such a way that they would be attracted to the irresistible usefulness of engaging a professional organizer.

As I prepared, it occurred to me that most of the people I work with are in the uncluttering business in some way. Aren't many of us looking to simplify lives and clarify meaning for others in our realm of expertise? This includes not only enlightened entrepreneurs but also therapists, coaches, energy workers, spirit guides, and other healing practitioners. So how do you translate a masterful one-on-one skill, such as one-on-one counseling or office organization, to communicating with groups about what you can do for them? As I suggested to the professional organizers, the key is to keep it simple and keep it personal. The people who hire you are those who feel attuned with you and enjoy the pleasure of your company. So, open with a story that reflects your own vulnerability and your passion to serve. Talk to one person at a time and not to the group as a whole. Speak conversationally, as you would over coffee. Allow silences. Apply your ability to declutter lives and spaces to the content of your talk.

Invitation—Consider how in your work, current or past, you've been in the "uncluttering business." In the mirror (aloud or silently), or in turns with your relational presence partner, reflect on this.

10. Some Tips on Preparing to Speak

I had a lifelong habit of overpreparing for talks until I discovered that being relationally present with my audience allows me to think on my feet beyond what I could have imagined.

—Michelle Veneziano, osteopathic physician

Find Heaven on Stage

> I don't like to commit myself about heaven and hell—you see, I have friends in both places.
> —Mark Twain

A childhood of suffering unmet connection often leads to a lifetime pattern of either craving attention or avoiding it at all costs. Self-consciousness is epidemic in modern society. No wonder it drives so many people nuts to be the center of attention and be expected to speak. I was that way for nearly fifty years.

These days, when I stand in front of a group, I see brave and true humans who are each fighting a hard battle. I see worthy folks who crave connection but would rather not show their neediness. And I know that many people out there are hurting, even in the most well-off crowds. I've learned that the one thing they can all do on cue is take me up on an invitation for authentic connection, thus creating a sense of belonging for them, and heaven on stage for me.

You may have heard the allegory about the difference between Heaven and Hell. In Hell there are rows of tables laden with sumptuous food, but the diners are moaning in hunger because they have spoons with five-foot-long handles strapped to their arms and thus are unable to bring the food to their mouths. In Heaven it's the same setup of delicious meals and too-long utensils, but the people have learned to feed each other across the table.

This is an apt metaphor for relational presence. Rather than trying to connect with our audience by forcibly bringing them to us, when we nourish our listeners with kind attention, heavenly connection happens naturally.

> **Invitation**—Consider allegory about Heaven and Hell on the preceding page. In the mirror (aloud or silently), or in turns with your relational presence partner, reflect on how it relates to your life or how you view life here on earth.

Slow Down Time in Consciousness

> *It would be an advantage for anyone to make everything appear to move in slow motion. It would give you time to analyze the situation and the actions of everyone and everything around you. It gives you extra time to determine your actions in a pressure situation. This would be incredibly useful in business, driving your car in traffic, playing games, military combat, sports and life-threatening situations.*
>
> —Enoch Tan, "How to Slow Down Time with Your Mind"

Anything worth doing is worth doing slowly.
—Mae West

In thirty years facilitating Speaking Circles, I have been guiding people to master the skill of slowing down time in front of groups. Speaking anxiety activates the flight or freeze responses, so how can you possibly be articulate when your mind alternates between racing and stalled and you feel like everyone can see right through you? I lived with that misery into my late forties, when I developed the exercise of being in front of a supportive group for finite periods of time as I practiced presence with one person at a time without even having to speak. From here, participants found themselves able to breathe, slow their mind, and allow the appropriate words to arise naturally.

Effective leaders in all realms know how to slow down time in their mind to bring out the best in themselves and others in the many opportunities for mindfulness each day brings. The direct way to develop the capacity to slow down time is through regular meditation or other stillness practice, and perhaps this is what many effective leaders are able to do. But I believe that the majority of them don't have the time, inclination, or capacity to sustain such a practice.

So I want you to know that the organic way to slow down time and facilitate a sense of ease in any room is to patiently be with one listener at a time so *they* feel seen.

When I slow down within myself while being with another, I naturally drop into the deeper waters under my mind's chatter.
—Lynne Velling,
SCI Director of Facilitator Programs

> **Invitation**—Here's an exercise from chapter 1. It would be interesting to see if this time around you have a different experience with it, assuming you've read more since then and done other exercises: Take at least a minute in the mirror, or one-minute turns with a relational presence practice partner, to talk more slowly than usual about how it feels to talk slowly.

See Public Speaking as Energy Transformation

Anxiety in front of groups—from unease to terror—is the inevitable result of the unexamined assumption that public speaking is *"me trying to get through to them."* This assumption exists because it is how public speaking is conventionally taught and practiced. But audiences do not respond well to presenters who place a higher priority on delivering information than they do on sensing and honoring the energy in the room.

For a glimpse into the model of public speaking as energy transformation, imagine you are an acupuncturist, chiropractor, or therapist who has built a solid one-on-one practice. You are presented with golden opportunities to speak at association or educational meetings. Not comfortable in front of groups, you attend conventional trainings where the assumption is that public speaking is a skill unrelated to the one-on-one mastery you already have. You utilize techniques that help you cope on the surface, but authenticity is compromised.

The alternative is to see public speaking as energy transformation, where one-on-one proficiency in any field can be transmitted to groups without you needing to learn new techniques. Just as your work with an individual flows effortlessly and intuitively from presence and breath, your words to a group can also achieve that effortless flow. Once you access this group-aligned place within you, public speaking becomes a new universe.

From here, you get to *be* in the comfort zone of your mastery instead of just talking about it. The acupuncturist penetrates points in the group energy body as precisely with words as with needles. The chiropractor opens and adjusts the audience body. The therapist "listens a group into existence" with the same expansive attention they provide a client.

Be the most passionate person in the room. Your energy and vibe will lift others as well.
—Hiral Nagda

This model extends to any practice founded on one-on-one proficiency, and to individuals in any field who have good one-on-one rapport.

> **Invitation**—Think of a profession, sport, or creative area in which you have excellent one-on-one proficiency. In the mirror (aloud or silently), or in turns with a relational presence practice partner, reflect on how you might talk to a group about that skill while physically embodying it in some way.

Practice Vocal Freedom Play

The creation of something new is not accomplished by the intellect, but by the play-instinct acting from inner necessity.
— C.G. Jung

In 2017 I initiated a program called Vocal Freedom Play (VFP) with the aim of loosening the vocal cords and minds of speakers by opening up the full range of their voices, in expressions that were essentially gibberish, unadulterated by thinking. You see, you can't do gibberish and think at the same time. Back then I did VFP duets with folks who liked to sing out loud as well as some who were anxious about singing when anyone else was around. As children, many had heard and internalized criticisms like "Your voice hurts my ears" or "You can't carry a tune so just be quiet." But in VFP, they found they had fun since, among other things, it has no requirement to carry a tune or remember any words, and there's no shame in the game.

Back then I didn't have the courage to follow through on a program that would publicly expose my own imperfect voice. I also discovered that some folks feel uncomfortable even *hearing* gibberish, so I discontinued the program after a few months. But there's something about becoming an octogenarian that makes me no longer care much what others think, because this is so much fun for me and I know it can be of value and pleasure for many.

At my 80th birthday celebration, I led the guests in an ecstatic experience—at least for me. With drums and clapping, they kept a strong beat while I soloed over with gibberish. As you'll hear in the video referenced in the Invitation below, I exclaimed, "That's the most fun I ever had!"

> **Invitation**—On YouTube, search for "Vocal Freedom Play." The 9-minute video starts at my 80th birthday party and flashes back in time to a variety of scenes from 6 years before with duets and small groups that demonstrate VFP games. The video also presents opportunities for you to sing along, and perhaps will inspire you to share it with friends and play some of the games together.

Appreciate Being an Introvert

Authentic connection with an audience is easier for us introverts because we are allergic to performance, so our natural magnetism is not compromised by façade. When you can recognize your introversion as a public speaking strength rather than weakness, you can plug into a natural capacity to set a calm pace that facilitates an irresistible "field of belonging" in

In a gentle way, you can shake the world.
—Mahatma Gandhi

I have come to see that the gentle kindness of my presence enlivens audiences by interweaving our energies.

—Nancy Montier, life coach

a room. You can bring an audience to that place in the first minute; simply take a full breath (or two) with them and start conversationally with a one- or two-minute personal story that segues into why you are speaking to them that day.

In front of a group, you can learn to be yourself out loud while coming in soft with your content and a message that serves your audience. You don't have to alter your essential nature. Magnetism and dynamism are both good qualities in a speaker. Those who lead with dynamism, though, are at a disadvantage in that it requires them to continuously stream energy out to their listeners. Introverts are better equipped to be naturally magnetic because we let the audience energetically come to *us*, like iron filings to a magnet.

If you are a natural dynamo, practice entering the engagement more like a magnet. Once you've established attunement with a group you can let your dynamism show up organically.

If you are an introvert, your work is to allow attunement with an audience to happen naturally. From there you will notice that elements of dynamism show up through the passion you have around your information and your message.

If, as an introvert, you believe that it will be more difficult for you to overcome your anxiety around public speaking than others who may appear to be more confident than you are, never fear. Most of my Speaking Circles participants over the years have been introverts. I have found that for the most part facilitating an introvert into relational presence with listeners is easier than guiding a dynamo to go back to beginner's mind to establish attunement.

> **Invitation**—Are you more a dynamo or a magnet? Take at least a minute in the mirror (aloud or silently), or one-minute turns with a relational presence practice partner, to reflect on how this essay landed with you.

Facilitate a Soulful Space

In *A Hidden Wholeness: The Journey Toward an Undivided Life* (2009), educator Parker Palmer writes:

> *In this culture, we know how to create spaces that invite the intellect to show up, to argue its case, to make its point. We know how to create spaces that invite the emotions to show up, to express anger or joy. We know how to create spaces that invite the will to show up, to consolidate effort and energy around a common task. And we surely know how to create spaces that invite the ego to show up, preening itself and claiming its turf! But we seem to know very little about creating spaces that invite the soul to show up, this core of ourselves, our selfhood.*

Creating space that systematically invites the soul to show up in groups is the domain of social architecture. A social architect is one who designs and facilitates social interactions with a predetermined goal in mind. One recognized social architect of the previous century was Bill Wilson, instrumental in the founding of Alcoholics Anonymous in 1937. His wife Lois co-founded Al-Anon in 1951. These organizations are still going strong today because a masterful social architect

When I let my presence be a magnet for the inner light of my listeners, sparks start flying.

—Nancy Montier

was there through the rough going to facilitate the developing protocol for AA. (The inside joke at the time was about the hell it is to get a hundred drunks to agree on anything.)

Bill W., as he was known, shepherded the crafting of the Twelve Steps and Twelve Traditions that leave no loopholes for anyone to co-opt or otherwise divert the movement, break the format, or distract the group from its mission to help those who suffer. These Steps and Traditions have a rich and enduring importance in society, and many other groups have gone on to embrace the tenets and format that Bill W. established.

My recovery experiences in Overeaters Anonymous influenced my path to Speaking Circles, which is my own contribution as a social architect. OA exposed me to AA history and, among others, the principles of no crosstalk and not getting involved in other people's content. Relational presence practice applies these principles to working through public speaking anxiety. And when the struggle is over, most keep coming back for what could be considered "Stage 3 Recovery," where their path is to bring more and more relational presence into their daily lives.

> **Invitation**—Bill Wilson wrote, "The feeling of having shared in a common peril is one element in the powerful cement which binds us." In the mirror (aloud or silently), or in turns with your relational presence partner, reflect on your experience with others in dealing with a common peril.

11.

In the First Minutes of Your Talk

At a training, Lee handed out champagne glasses and pretended to carefully pour some into each glass. He noted that if you were serving champagne, you would be mindful, making sure each guest was ready to receive it. You wouldn't spritz it around the room and all over them. From the first minute of every talk, I remember this apt metaphor and pour my words accordingly.

—Linda Graf, relationship coach

Take Your All-Important Opening Breath
Co-authored with Doreen Downing

Create space simply to "be" and clarity emerges for you to see.
—Gabriella Goddard

You have been introduced to the audience and they have welcomed you with applause. And now there is a moment that can be anxiety producing for many: it's quiet. And it's important. The silence between the end of the applause and the first words out of your mouth is a critical time in rapport building and you cannot get that opportunity back once you start to speak. Something special happens in a room when the speaker is willing to come to a complete rest for a breath or two. When you take the time to let your feet sink deeply into the earth, they will feel the ground underneath them too.

This is the time when you communicate that you are also listening, not just speaking. When they realize you are truly there with them—and *for* them—a subtle energy shift happens in the room. As you model what paying real attention looks and feels like, many will find themselves listening deeply before you have said a word. But to do this, you must be willing to stand in the stillness.

This meeting place of two worlds, yours and theirs, is where you gently join. This is the beginning of a relationship where you communicate that they are invited to co-create an experience with you. The effectiveness of the message you are there to share with them can only happen when the listeners are tuned in; and for this to happen, you must tune into them first. They may be sitting there with expectations, hopes, prejudices, distractions, and judgments, but instead of meeting them at that superficial edge of evaluation, you enter into the vast, silent Now. When you master this revolutionary act of listening, you are able to transform the narrower energy of intellect into their willingness to join you.

This is where you and your audience make an unspoken agreement that something real is about to happen, that you are including them in the journey, that their presence has weight. You are coming into real time with them, the pace at which people get to genuinely know each other. You have communicated that you are not in a hurry, that simply being together is what matters first.

This expanding moment together is a demonstration of your commitment to being open to intimacy. You are revealing yourself in human form, no masks, no pretenses. Stripped of words, gestures, and performance technique, you stand in the fullness of relational presence. We are often asked: "How much time should I take in silence?" or "Won't they get uncomfortable?" In certain environments, this will be as little as one full breath; in others it can stretch to several breaths. And yes, some may get a bit uncomfortable, but if you are okay with it, they will soon be okay with it as well.

A full breath before speaking lets me connect with what I truly want to say from my heart, not just my head.
—Ellen Schermerhorn, HR professional

> **Invitation**—In the mirror (aloud or silently), or taking turns with your relational presence partner, take two full, easy, luxurious breaths, like the ones you would take in front of an audience of 1,000 before saying a word, and reflect on how that was for you.

> Don't be afraid to let your heart beat strong and loud in a room full of silence. Your heart beats for a reason, woman!
> —Ayokunle Falomo

Let Your Heart Pound

I suffered deer-in-the-headlights stage fright for decades. The shame ran deep. All I wanted was to manage the terror, but nothing helped until I devised relational presence practice. Then a few years later, in my mid-fifties, I had an epiphany.

I was being introduced by Glenna Salsbury, president of the National Speakers Association, to give my first presentation at our national convention. Hundreds of my peers—professional speakers and other speaking coaches among them—were sitting in wait out there.

As I was being introduced, my heart was pounding big time. THUMP! THUMP! THUMP! Each beat a seismic event. But each thump gave me an electric surge of . . . pleasure!

It was then that I fully understood that the symptoms of stage fright are exactly the same as those of intense excitement. Heart beating out of one's chest, shaky knees, and a blank mind. Without negative interpretation, these are not problems at all.

What a miracle in my life was that realization! And what joy to facilitate this transformation in others.

> **Invitation**—Imagine being introduced to give a talk to a large group. Your heart is pounding, but you feel fine because you no longer have a negative interpretation about that. In the mirror (aloud or silently), or taking turns with your relational presence partner, reflect on how this shift could have occurred.

"Let Go of Your Face"

The words came to me while observing a Speaking Circles newcomer struggling mightily to cope with extreme self-consciousness while maintaining a strained smile. When I asked if she was willing to take some coaching she nodded yes, and I suggested: "Let go of your face." Her strained smile instantly dissolved, her eyes softened, and she breathed deeply. The transformation held as she continued her turn. She had no idea how rigidly she'd been holding her face, and the gentle invitation was all she needed to notice and let it go. At the next Circle she talked about how letting go of her face had been beneficial in sensitive communications with her family.

Let go of your face is one of those directions that transmits something directly to the body without having to be understood or resisted by the mind. When you release your face you "get out of your head" and are better able to source your essential knowing. Right now, as you are reading this, what happens when you contemplate the suggestion to let go of your face and breathe? Do you feel something drop away, as I just did when I typed it?

I do not have to give any further explanation about how to do it. Everyone has their own way of holding their face, and when given the suggestion everyone knows instinctively how to relax it.

Why does this instruction work so well? In this world of appearances, which are of course deceiving, we humans tend to identify with our face as if it represents who we really

> *Some of us think holding on makes us strong; but sometimes it is letting go.*
> —Hermann Hesse

are. On it we carry our image, our reputation, the person we take ourselves to be. When we're the center of attention we may unconsciously hold subtle tension around our eyes and mouth, which become a Bermuda Triangle of constriction.

The organic process of dissolving self-consciousness and coming into one's power in the world can start with the small surge of relief that results from noticing the habit of holding tension in the face. Next time you are in front of a mirror, invite yourself to *let go of your face*. And just see—and feel—what happens!

> **Invitation**—In the mirror (aloud or silently), or taking turns with your relational presence partner, start by letting go of your face, and reflect on the place in which you landed.

Turn Your "Ums" into "Yums"
Co-authored with Doreen Downing

Linguists call them "filler words" and they appear to go in fashions. In current usage, "um" is overtaking "er" as the filler of choice.
—Oliver Moody

"Ums" and "uhs" seem ingrained for many. In some performance-oriented public speaking programs, "ums" are clicked and counted. This is a behavioral approach that works for some by breaking the habit through negative reinforcement. However, we see a bigger picture, having come to believe that every "um" and "uh" (along with each "and" and "so" that patch together run-on sentences) are exactly the places where speakers give away their power. And thus can be reversed to enhance the moment.

Here is how you would eliminate "ums" in relational presence practice. You first become aware you are saying them, and then, whenever you hear yourself say "um," you replace it with "yum." The playfulness of this approach makes for a more effective learning environment than hearing a clicker go off informing you of your transgression.

The places these filler words come from are precisely where our attachment to content makes us contract. They are the points where we have the choice instead to *expand* our presence. The "um" presents an opportunity at the heart of our work. Much of what is written about filler words regards them as unconscious habits. The sounds, words, and phrases that fill up the silences are for the most part not even recognized by people as they speak. "Unconscious" means "out of awareness." When a habit is repeated without conscious awareness, we can guess that there is also a reason for that habit that is not yet identified or understood.

Filler sounds keep people safe from stumbling and getting lost, safe from the consequences of making a mistake in public. Whatever reason, conscious or not, when an "um" is uttered, it is a signal that anxiety is lurking. People are more comfortable saying "um" than just being in the stillness of relational presence. Stepping into the silence and letting go of the filler takes courage.

Trying to eliminate the "ums" and "uhs" without first understanding their personal significance can be difficult. It is also a missed opportunity to transform fear into powerful transmission. To consciously choose to face one's fear is bold

That "um" is our mouth's way of saying to our listeners, "Hey, I've still got the stage here. I'll be right back with that information. Just gimme a second. It's NOT your turn to talk yet."
—Jeff Davenport

and beautiful. As fear dissolves and fillers disappear, potent presence shows up and does the talking.

> **Invitation**—Have you had or do you have a problem with filler words? In the mirror, or taking turns with your relational presence partner, reflect on that. And think about turning "ums" into "yums."

Heal Your Relationship with Audiences

I've long resisted calling my work a "healing" modality, nor have I identified myself as a healer. But recently it was called to my attention that healing one's relationship with audiences is precisely what this work is about. As an agent of such transformation, I have come to recognize Speaking Circles facilitators as healers. Years ago, I was struck by these words I read in *Utne Reader* magazine: "Healers, whether they are doctors or shamans, are able to heal (as opposed to merely cure) through a deep mutuality with their patients—through the potent magic of fellow feeling. Healers assist us to heal ourselves by enhancing our natural healing processes."

While keeping to the spirit of that definition, I want to go beyond doctors and shamans to include a variety of other healing agents who've shown up at Speaking Circles. We've had educators, coaches, trainers, therapists, energy workers, and wellness practitioners of all varieties. Then there are healing agents in fields that may not seem conducive to it, such as financial advisers who help heal clients around their

---

Healing may not be so much about getting better, as about letting go of everything that isn't you—all of the expectations, all of the beliefs—and becoming who you are.

—Rachel Naomi Remen

My work as a real estate agent reaches its highest level when I'm able to match clients with homes that contain and inspire them. This process is facilitated by my listening and seeing them on the deepest level.

— Nadine Greenwood

relationship with money. There are real estate agents, lawyers, and others in realms that are fraught with high anxiety who bring consciousness of the healing process to their work.

Many a professional delivers expert services in their field. But those who are healing agents do even more; they communicate their expertise from a mindset of kind regard that shows up in their listening eyes and makes for easy connection. Common among true healers in all fields is their habit of seeing others so they feel seen in their wholeness. Such professional capacity opens the client's essential being to the change the healer represents.

There are true healers in every family, workplace, and circle of friends. Perhaps you are one, or you feel you have been called to move in the direction of becoming a more conscious agent of healing energy. The healer evokes an energy field of clarity and wholeness that nurtures the sense that anything is possible. This is the portal through which healers in any area enter each interaction. The capacity to hold stillness and presence for others is the essential practice of relational presence, and in every realm of usefulness it is the quality of the space you hold for others that is precisely where the alchemy of healing kicks in.

My heart goes out to the many healers and potential healers out there who do not yet know that speaking to a group calls for precisely the same quality of attention that brings flow to their one-on-one interactions. I want them to know that they can heal their relationship with any audience by holding stillness, presence, and space with one person at a time.

Natural forces within us are the true healers of disease.
—Hippocrates

Healing social trauma is an under-discussed phenomenon in psychotherapy. Relational presence practice healed 40 years of social shame for me.
—Maurice Taylor, psychotherapist

> **Invitation**—Whatever field you are in, reflect on some aspect of healing that your work calls you to provide to others. In the mirror (aloud or silently), or in turns with your relational presence partner, see if you can talk about yourself, in some respect, as an agent of healing.

Don't Look for Audience Approval

Care about what other people think and you will always be their prisoner.
—Lao Tzu

It is common for anxious speakers to project boredom and disengagement onto neutral faces in the audience. When there are no smiles or nods it's easy to read disinterest. But we don't really know what's going on for them. I asked Speaking Circle afficionados around the world for their take on looking for audience approval, and received these responses.

Alex Martynov, leadership coach in Prague, told me:

When the need to please the listeners goes away, one has no choice but to face oneself, to tap into some place inside and be present to what is emerging from there.

Eric Atwood, Speaking Circles facilitator in San Rafael, California, wrote:

We can never know what an audience is thinking simply by looking at them. If you are with one person in an audience who you can tell is not with you, you don't need to continue engaging with them. Simply move on to a person who is there with you. Your job is not to engage every single person in the room. Indeed, there are almost always people who are checked out in any public speaking setting, and you cannot coerce them to engage with you. Your job is to engage with the people who are with you. When you fully engage with those who are engaged with you, you'll sense the same energy arising from others in the room without you even looking at them.

John Dawson, Speaking Circles facilitator in Bristol, England, wrote:

Audiences are passive listeners; they are not conversational listeners. They don't nod very much or smile. This is normal, but lots of speakers can get freaked out by blank faces, even when they give blank faces themselves when they are in the audience. We just do it naturally.

The pressure to perform and the compulsion to please naturally dissolve in a safe container of unconditional support.
—Lea Bayles,
holistic success coach

Sean Vanonckelen, Speaking Circles facilitator in Belgium, is a wedding ceremony officiant who marries dozens of couples a year and shares their story with the guests. He wrote:

One audience might be laughing and crying, another audience might look at me with blank faces for a full hour. Very often these blank faces come up to me afterwards to say how much they enjoyed what I said. Ever since I stopped feeling responsible for how people feel and react during the ceremony, I can truly do what I love most: share stories in a unique and authentic way.

Imagine being in the audience of the Dalai Lama and you are mesmerized. But if you look around, you'll see a sea of blank faces in which you could read disinterest. You see, when a speaker is making great sense, most folks are intently listening and applying the stories and information to their own lives. They are not of a mind to signal the Dalai Lama that he is doing a good job. Nor to signal you. That's why in relational presence practice we ask the group to listen with a soft, steady gaze of kind regard and not reassure with smiles or nods.

One Speaking Circles participant related to this notion, and in her turn talked about how her husband shows enthusiastic interest in the teachings she shares with him; so with him she continues to flow and express herself creatively. But, she said, when speaking to groups at work:

> *I've tended to perceive disinterest on their faces that makes me think I'm not saying anything new they don't already know. I would make myself small, and my creative flow would stop because of what I perceived out there. In relational presence practice I'm learning to allow my listeners to be as they are and not imagine what they think of me, since I want to speak with the conviction that reflects how I feel. I have things to share, we all do, and I'm looking forward to allowing more and more of what's inside of me to come out.*

Invitation—Consider: Is there someone in your life you look to for approval more than you think is healthy? You might talk to yourself in the mirror about this, aloud or silently, or take turns talking about it with your relational presence partner.

Tap Into Generosity of Spirit

> *We are constantly sharing our consciousness with others; it actually takes an effort to freeze someone out, which involves keeping your consciousness tightly wound and contracted. Generosity of spirit is real, and we experience it in shared moments of love, compassion, and empathy.*
>
> —Deepak Chopra

Clarity and candor are essential in times of crisis—and so is generosity of spirit.
—Jon Meacham

Humanity has always suffered dire crises, whether personal, family, cave, or country. Our current existential climate crisis, along with the attendant political and social calamities, is perilous to the quality of all life on the planet. This is a global quagmire that many millions more have in common than any crisis heretofore in human history.

I am here to point out that sometimes in dire circumstances the only thing left to work with is . . . our own attitude. After seven decades of periodic utter confusion about what I'm doing here on earth, a clue recently came to me. My mind isolated the most useful quality of humans to nurture and spread. That quality is *generosity of spirit*.

I see generosity of spirit as a tenderly precise vibration of shared humanity radiated naturally by many and resisted by some. Donating materially to causes or with one's time may arise from generosity of spirit, but the quality does not imply giving away one's resources. Generosity of spirit is a pure state of being seen in eyes that are prone to twinkle. It is a generous outlook exuded without words; and when there are words, the spirit shows up underneath the content, right from the opening seconds of a talk or a personal conversation.

Any two or more people with strong generosity of spirit (even speakers of different languages) will have a naturally pleasurable interaction upon meeting. Relationships, whether business or pleasure, are best sustained when each has a strong spirit of generosity. And humans with generosity of spirit naturally uplift those who are liftable.

Deepak Chopra writes in a 2021 article on his website, "The Generosity of Spirit: A Breakthrough":

> *When the generosity of spirit fails us, or we fail it, conflicts develop. Consciousness pulls itself in like a turtle retreating into its shell. Then in isolation all kinds of peculiar, hostile, negative ideas fester "in here." The violent loner is a prisoner of constricted, isolated awareness that has lost the capacity to share in the generosity of spirit that keeps society going.*

More than ever, we earthlings need a shared consciousness of generosity of spirit to hold us together through these turbulent times.

Invitation—Reflect on how your own generosity of spirit shows up in your relationships. You might talk to yourself in the mirror about this, aloud or silently, or take turns exploring it with your relational presence partner.

12.

Maintaining Presence Throughout the Talk

Once I discovered that my words were found in other people's eyes, I stopped worrying ahead of time about what I'm going to say. I've never again been in my former hell-state of talking in front of a group. Without this transformation I would not have ended up in the center of the life I now live, as an artist, teacher, and thought leader.

—Cara Brown, artist and teacher

> *A lot of times, rather than helping people with horse problems, I'm helping horses with people problems.*
> —Buck Brannaman

Be an Audience Whisperer

The 2011 film *Buck* is a documentary about the man who inspired Robert Redford's 1998 movie *The Horse Whisperer*. Buck Brannaman believes that there is no reason ever to "break" a horse. He holds that a horse's fears and mental processes can be recognized and gently neutralized without the need for confrontation.

The notion of needing to "break" a wild mustang for its own good has long been an assumption in our culture. It occurs to me that I grew up with a similar assumption around speaking in public: that high anxiety around it must be vanquished head-on, through sheer force of will.

Many come to Speaking Circles having punished themselves with that mindset for years, and it doesn't make sense to them at first that having the gentle space to *experience* the anxiety and have it witnessed is far more effective than trying to learn behavioral strategies to "bring it under control." But soon they learn, through practice, to achieve *attunement* with an audience, an effortless state of *being* from which *doing*—speaking—arises naturally and articulately.

After seeing *Buck* I was honored to provide public speaking training to a group of practitioners who apply the healing power of horses as transformational agents for at-risk youth and other populations in need. Many of the equines doing this work were rescued from lives lived under the old paradigm of control. When I was taken to visit these sentient beings and stood next to one with no agenda but to share the stillness, I profoundly felt her presence as if from the center of the earth.

Although horses do this without eye contact, my work with the practitioners began with the understanding that the ecstatic attunement they already have with horses can be extended to human audiences through a warm, non-effortful gaze. My promise was that when they learn this gaze of attunement and practice it with groups, they would become *audience whisperers*, and their listeners would follow them anywhere.

> **Invitation**—Remember an animal with whom you have experienced deep connection, whether a horse, a cat, a dog, a bird, a turtle, a hamster. Talk to yourself in the mirror about the nature of that connection or take turns exploring it with your relational presence partner.

Communicate Vertically

By ordinary observation, our planet Earth is flat. By similar appearances, the audience's attention occupies a horizontal plane. Many an experienced presenter has bought into this assumption, which has them sweeping the room side to side like the beam from a lighthouse. But covering an audience from this horizontal orientation fosters separation in a room. This is because energetically each listener occupies a personal line of gravity down to the center of the earth and up into the cosmos.

When you communicate from a vertical orientation, you align with your listeners' seven energy chakras and thus

Gravity wins over all other known forces.
—Andrea M. Ghez

become a magnet for connection. I mean this literally since our essential attraction is from our own center of gravity down to the center of the earth. We don't connect with an audience by *trying* to connect, since such effort comes from a mindset of separateness. But as each of us is powerfully attracted from our center of gravity in a straight line down to the center of the earth, where we all energetically meet, we merely need to recognize that we are *already* connected.

Imagine starting a talk by standing in stillness up front while sensing your presence flowing down your arms and legs to the center of the earth. You don't get your audience to join you down there by "grabbing" them with your eyes or your smile. All that is required is a soft, steady gaze of kind regard. Human magnetism is simply about allowing nature to take its course. You don't flit horizontally from face to face making fleeting eye contact. You square up eye-to-eye, heart-to-heart, metaphorically belly-to-belly with one individual at a time. In this way you align with the unity of all beings. When your words arise naturally from the underground connection, they seem to resonate down into the earth and *up* through your listeners' beings.

> **Invitation**—Stand, breathe easy, and let your energy drop down as if to the center of the earth. Stay standing as you communicate to yourself in the mirror, aloud or silently about how this feels. Or stand face-to-face with your relational presence partner and take turns reflecting on what it feels like to let gravity have its way with you.

Practice Sustainable Communication

Sustainable communication simply asks that we do not exhaust our resources. The most valuable natural resource in any room is the listening. Your audience is a living, breathing, interconnected field of seething vitality, creativity, sensitivity, intelligence, beauty, and value. They are pulsing with life, crave good-natured adventure, and treasure a well-facilitated learning environment.

The way to master sustainable communication is to develop your capacity to refresh and renew your listeners rather than exhaust them. You do this by not talking *at* them or *to* them, but *with* them, and to allow being quiet together when there is nothing to say. This calls on you to make it easy for them to be with you and listen to you. This is done by speaking (or being silent) with one person at a time, seeing them so they feel seen.

The practice is like going to the gym; but rather than building up your physical muscles, you are developing the muscle of interpersonal power. This is a gym that generates more pleasure than pain, and along the way self-consciousness and performance anxiety—even severe stage fright—naturally melt away.

The other important natural resource in the room to consider is your Self and its relationship to the vertical energy discussed in the previous section. By becoming proficient at plugging your feet (and sometimes your seat) into planet Earth, you allow yourself to be recharged with the vital energy

I've learned that people will forget what you said, people will forget what you did, but people will never forget how you made them feel.
—Maya Angelou

of Life. This underground infusion allows you to be held and inspired by your listeners. Your energy is renewed even as you speak, and thus your communication is sustained and sustainable.

> **Invitation**—Stand, breathe easy, locate a sense of speaking anxiety within, and imagine it dropping down through your arms and legs and melting away. Stay standing as you talk to yourself in the mirror (aloud or silently) about how this feels. Or stand face-to-face with your Relational Presence partner and take turns reflecting on how this feels.

13.

Bringing Relational Presence into Everyday Life

Earl and Doreen Downing have been a couple for twenty-two years and married for fourteen. Doreen, Training Director of Speaking Circles International, has facilitated hundreds of Circles that Earl has attended. The next page is a discussion regarding their experience with relational presence.

— Earl Downing and Doreen Downing, author of
The 7 Secrets to Essential Speaking

Discussion Regarding Relational Presence

Doreen: The soft, steady gaze of kind regard we train listeners to give to the person up front is exactly what's required for a sustainable romantic relationship. Earl and I know precisely how to give each other space to be exactly who we are, beyond judgment and expectations.

Earl: You know, when bad things happen for me during the day, I can't wait for Doreen to get home so I can get her listening. And when good things happen, I can't wait to share the joy. The great listener I see in the Circles is the same loving listener I see at home.

Doreen: When we have some kind of conflict, sometimes one of us feels we are not being heard and calmly says, "You're not listening to me." The other knows precisely what that means and immediately adjusts. As a psychologist, in my work with couples I find that those words often escalate the fight. With us, those words keep the peace.

Earl: Exactly. There's a whole different quality of listening that we know is possible for us and that we depend on. Sometimes that quality is not there because we've got our own little point of view, and we get a little bit of conflict. But we've become masters at letting it go with love and listening.

Words that Must Be Said

After 30 years leading listener-friendly public speaking classes and certifying others globally to follow suit, the realization struck me that my life's work is not about public speaking *(Gulp)*.... My life's work is about private listening and responsible sharing. It's about clarity of intention and getting out of one's own way with words.

Public speaking is a lively wing of my interest, but it is just one application of embodied relational presence with self and others. The deeper spirit of my calling is about connecting our hard-earned inner wisdom and unexpressed love with words that must be said, in private and in public.

To come boldly from shared stillness and loving kindness calls for listening first, whether home or at work, in the boardroom or the bedroom. Above all, my intention is to model self-care and community care. Our species is in its infancy as social beings. In these chaotic times, many of us are finding healthy ways to soothe our ravaged nervous systems and toddle toward shaky inner peace. And perhaps move toward reconciliation with *what is* out there in the world.

Now is the time to drop the guise and level with ourselves and others. Now is the time for tough love, saturated with kindness. Now is the time to be present to the miracle of life within and around us. This is my work going forward.

> *When things start to fall apart in your life, you feel as if your whole world is crumbling. But actually it's your fixed identity that's crumbling. And that's cause for celebration.*
>
> —Pema Chodron

Invitation—Is there someone in your life who can use some tough love from you? You might talk to yourself in the mirror about this (aloud or silently) or take turns exploring it with your relational presence partner.

Let Muscle Memory Kick In

Practice puts brains in your muscles.
—Sam Snead

Takahiro Kurata is a certified Speaking Circles facilitator in Tokyo who has come to see relational presence practice as a kind of martial art. He writes:

> *When I was in high school and a certified black belt, for three years I practiced "Kyudo," the Japanese art of archery. I sat in the Dojo training hall in front of a target that was 28 meters away. For the first three months I was not allowed to shoot arrows at the target. I trained myself to breathe, concentrate on the target, and wait to shoot the arrow until the body is in such a relaxed state that the arrow releases almost on its own.*
>
> *It was very boring, my legs were often in pain, and I wondered if this was really necessary. Why couldn't I just pick up a bow and practice shooting at the target? After three months of this, I found that my mind was what is called "Heijyoshin." I was calm, not too excited, not over-confident nor in self-doubt. My mind was ready to focus on the target without being interrupted by unnecessary noise, such as thoughts. I realized that three months of just sitting in front of the target had trained me to develop muscle memory so that when I picked up the bow and arrow I could behave and think automatically when facing the target.*
>
> *Similarly, with Relational Presence I breathe and settle into a natural connection with the audience (my*

The key to martial art is "Don't fight, invite."
—Taka Kurata, Lean Six Sigma Master Black Belt

> target), *for as long as it takes. From here, meaningful content and soothing silences tend to arise naturally.*
>
> *Martial art is named "Dou" in Japanese. Dou is translated to "way, path or road." It is a way of learning. Beginners learn simple patterned motions, called "Kata," that they repeat until those simple motions become muscle memory. I find a similarity between Dou and Relational Presence practice in terms of the learning process.*

Thank you, Taka-san! In relational presence practice, we train the *Kata* of breath and gaze in an energy field of shared stillness and kind regard that is at the core of human connection. Through repetitious turns in a group we develop something akin to muscle memory behind our eyes and in our breathing. The memory in this case is not literally in our muscles, but rather in our cerebral cortex. What we are remembering is how to stay relationally attuned to another at any moment. Inspired by Takahiro, I see relational presence as a martial art in which through repetition we learn body, mind, and soul how to invite connection with any audience, including an audience of one.

In the 1984 movie *The Karate Kid*, the student famously becomes proficient in the martial art through drilling and muscle memory. The 1948 book *Zen in the Art of Archery* by Eugen Herrigel shows us that repetition is key when we want actions to become more automatic and thus require less conscious effort so we can master whatever we are attempting to learn. Through mindful repetition we fine-tune our gaze to develop the subtle soft focus that allows us to shift our attention seamlessly between listeners, as the "muscle memory" of our well-practiced brain automatically makes instant calibrations as we go.

Through repetition we discover the natural synchrony of thinking and speaking while shifting focus between listeners. As we shift from person to person, our psyche automatically recalibrates the gaze to attune to each with nuances we cannot consciously grasp.

(See Part 3 of this book, The Zoom Revolution, for information on how muscle memory applies to virtual Speaking Circles.)

> **Invitation**—I imagine that most readers have mastered the complex skill of typing without thinking about what you are doing. That's pure muscle memory! If you are willing, would you type an email to me (lee@speakingcircles.com) about the great fortune and benefit of being a typing master?

Parenting from Relational Presence

There is no such thing as a perfect parent. So just be a real one.
—Sue Atkins

Developmental psychologists point out that the range of expression available to a child depends on the nature of the listening in their immediate environment. If the listening is receptive and respectfully curious, it evokes the full range of curiosity and wonder in the child. Listening from relational presence nourishes self-expression along with the capacity for adventure and discovery. The seeds of awareness emerge and bloom into full flower from the rich soil of expansive listening and shared stillness. This is a natural process.

The nature of consciousness is to reveal its multitudinous forms more fully when invited. However, children are limited in awareness and expression by the worldview of their parents and siblings, which informs what they are willing to hear. It is human, even for good listeners, to have an unconscious agenda that subtly closes off wide avenues of receptivity.

For some of us these closures were severe enough to make it dangerous to express ourselves at all. The relatively narrow listening available to many of us as children inhibited our potential, which still lives within us. Into adulthood, any group we faced instantly morphed into our family and we were terrified. Speaking Circles were originally conceived to provide support and guidance for a corrective emotional experience to reverse this history, and they have been effective to that end. But there is a side benefit, as well. Once performance anxiety falls away, the realization comes that we have found a safe arena in which to have as much unexpressed potential "listened out" as serves us.

What is the nature of the potential I'm talking about? The notion that we were each born with limitless possibilities does not here refer to specific capacities to become, say, a brain surgeon or a mountain climber or an orator. Rather, I mean that our true nature encompasses the full spectrum of essential human qualities. For instance, we each have within us the capacity to wake up every day to a new world of wonder. We are each inherently bright as the sun, luminous as a star, deep as the ocean, solid as

When I came to see the essential human connection no matter what their age, everything changed since I no longer engage in "top-down" parenting.
—Karen Aurit,
divorce mediation director

a redwood, spacious as the sky, and generous as the earth. We each come factory equipped to embody the grace of an eagle, the melody of a lark, and the heart of a lion. In essence, we are cuddly as kittens, loyal as Lassie, tender as the night, courageous as an astronaut, and peaceful as the Dalai Lama. And on and on.

To allow the full spectrum of essential human qualities to be listened out so that we can be aware of and embody more of each of them is beyond the capacity of a conventional nuclear family. It takes a certain kind of village to listen an individual into existence, and a Speaking Circle is that kind of village.

It is human nature to long for fulfillment of our potential, but the journey home often involves years of misdirection before we begin to recognize the realm in which that potential even exists. When we finally come to realize that true fulfillment lies in the realm of being rather than in the arena of doing, we become available to reunite with our essential qualities. And we are ready to elevate sweet listening to its rightful priority on this path—both in receiving it and in becoming luminous listeners for others on the journey.

Of course, it's the cosmic joke that when being assumes top priority over doing, grand achievements naturally and irresistibly manifest.

> **Invitation**—Remember or imagine how your range of expression was restricted growing up. Reflect on this to yourself in the mirror (aloud or silently), or by taking turns with your relational presence partner.

Parenting with Listening Eyes

From a mother in Wisconsin, shared with her permission:

Soon after I was introduced to relational presence practice, we were in the car, and my three-year-old daughter said, "Mommy, Mommy," and I said, "Yes, Diana?" And she said, "Mommy, Mommy!" and I said, "Yes?" Over and over, this happened. So I asked, "Diana, did you hear me say 'Yes'?" And she said, "Yeah, but Mommy, you are not looking at me."

That's when I realized for the first time that for her to feel heard and connect with me, she needs to feel like I'm giving her my listening eyes. It was an epiphany that was the foundation for what's happened the past year in my evolution as a mom. When my child feels like she's being treated like she has feelings and thoughts, and I'm really giving her my eyes, she softens. She wants to do what's being asked of her because there's harmony now in that space I'm creating. Everything used to be a battle, but now I have a different relationship with both of my daughters. I get ten times more hugs and kisses and instances of "I love you, Mommy."

The way we talk to our children becomes their inner voice.
—Peggy O'Mara

Relational Presence in Parenting a Special Needs Child

From a father in Oregon, shared with his permission:

Right before Covid started we discovered that our two-year-old son was on the autism spectrum. I thought then that there wasn't anything a parent wished for more than to have a healthy and normal child. This wasn't the life I'd planned,

A diagnosis can't predict the extraordinary love you will have for your child.
—Tara McCallan

I thought. I'd expected an ideal protégé to do things with me, like hunting and fishing. I went through a tough period. I struggled with my disappointment.

He was a happy boy and to this day he is still a happy boy, but I was dealing with him not living up to my expectations. I was wondering if we'd be able to go fly fishing someday, and would we be able to play catch. Those things seemed very remote then. We provided him with excellent special education and physical therapy. I also found Relational Presence practice quite helpful. You see, eye contact is not natural for people on the spectrum. Sometimes when I look into my son's eyes, he just doesn't seem to be there at all. But I know he's in there somewhere, processing on a different level.

I had to work with eye contact myself because it's something I avoided growing up, because of my own shame. My optimal way of connecting with my son no matter how vacant he seems to be is to take to his level and make my listening eyes softly available to him like we do for each other in Speaking Circles. I understand that he's being stimulated and overstimulated by so many different things in his environment, and I've come to see how meaningful it is in his world to have my eyes available as a place of stability. It's the soft, steady gaze of kind regard that gets him interested in what I have to say and lets me lift him out of whatever overstimulation he has going.

Being with his eyes is like physical refocusing. I sit down in front of him and take deep breaths and for a while he may not be there for me. I just sit and wait patiently for him to focus. I watch as his pupils go from the wide vacant setting to a narrower focus on me, and then I know he's there. I know he's responsive and ready to receive me, and he knows that I'm there too.

He's five going on six now. He's verbal, though he was delayed. He also has what is known as "splinter skills" in that he can tell you what 35 times 28 is in two seconds, but in contrast he still can't put on his own pants at this age. Socially, I see he doesn't always conform; for example, he laughs in an exaggerated way that draws stares from his peers.

We're really fortunate that he's got these splinter skills to work with, but he also has to work harder on his day-to-day stuff, his human interactions. He's come light years since the day we discovered that something was different about his world and how he processes. Before we knew he was on the spectrum I remember leaving the house to go on a business trip. I was trying to have a father-son interaction and I said, "Hey, sweetie pie, you know that Daddy is leaving." And he was vacant. He wasn't there at all. And I remember walking out the door and sobbing on the way to my business meeting because I thought something that I was doing was wrong.

Children on the spectrum often don't have an awareness of things going on around them. Early on, when I'd come home from work, I could come right up to him and he wouldn't have an awareness that I was there. He would just continue to go about what he was doing.

I often reflect that had I not discovered Relational Presence practice, how immensely different my experience would have been. Also, my own struggle may have continued to manifest without my own tools for interaction. Now when I get home, I get down to his level and gaze into his eyes, and I'm willing to wait a long time to allow him to focus on me. That gives me this connection with him I didn't have before. And he eventually responds, and that feels great.

> **Invitation**—Has there been a special needs child in your life? Talk to yourself in the mirror (aloud or silently) about your experience with this person or take turns with your relational presence partner reflecting on it.

Teaching from Connection

To be in connection with another human being a person needs to see the other and be seen by the other.

—Janet Surrey

Studies show that feeling seen in the classroom improves student learning outcomes. In her first book, *Caring: A Feminine Approach to Ethics and Moral Education* (1984), educator Nel Noddings writes about the relational nature of presence for a teacher in one-on-one interactions with a student, distinguishing it from the kind of connection found in more intimate relationships:

> *I do not need to establish a deep, lasting, time-consuming personal relationship with every student. What I must do is to be totally and non-selectively present to the student—to each student—as he addresses me. The time interval may be brief, but the encounter is total.*

My message to educators is that the practice of *teaching from connection* is a simple matter of expanding the percentage of classroom time in which you are truly seeing individual students through warm, available eyes, and letting them see you.

In bringing relational presence practice to faculty at Brigham Young University, Utah, I learned that even university professors experience public speaking anxiety. Some have it when addressing groups of their peers or out in the community. Sometimes it pops up in class when they are challenged by a situation. It has been gratifying to see that relational presence practice alleviates these issues. Jane Birch, Assistant Director for Faculty Development, Brigham Young University, wrote:

> *We invited Lee to help our professors open to their innate ability to connect at a visceral level to their students. He was able to demonstrate that this comes naturally to them when they drop their guard and see these young people as they are. Our research shows that students are seeking to know three things from their professors: Who are you? Who am I to you? And why does this course matter? The connection between the professor and student's eyes is the window through which the answers flow.*

Among the millions of educators out there from pre-K to university, many have been teaching for years in full and courageous presence. They are my heroes for their creative tightrope walking on the front lines of the real world of impressionable young people, day after day.

I vividly recall those of my own teachers, from kindergarten (seventy-five years ago!) through college, who made me

Tell me and I forget. Teach me and I may remember. Involve me and I learn.
—Benjamin Franklin

Feeling seen helps meet students' social and emotional needs and enhances their ability to learn.
—Niki Mott, educator

feel actually seen. Without their kind and intelligent regard, I would not have been able to do what I do in life, and I no longer take them for granted. Would you take a minute to recall some teachers who made a big difference in your life?

One who is currently making a difference in mine is Niki Mott, instructor of English and Rhetoric at New Mexico State University. Before her seventeen years teaching at the university level, she taught middle school for five years, high school for three, and was a middle school counselor for ten. After thirty-five years as an educator, she was inspired and influenced in her teaching by relational presence practice and became a certified Speaking Circles facilitator. She writes:

Our methods for communicating have changed so much, and yet we all still have a foundational need for connection. We have a basic need for being seen, for being acknowledged, and for being accepted.

It is clear to me that it is essential for educators to nurture students, which gives them a real sense of connection and encourages them to go on to graduate. In fact, it's said that if a student feels a connection with just one faculty or staff member, they tend to stay in school. Feeling "seen" in class, which is what relational presence practice offers them, can even work in large lecture classes, where they can otherwise feel like just a number. I prepare my students to go out into the world and become change agents, making contributions to the world. But before they can put themselves out there, they need to have the confidence of being understood, which we give them with our soft gaze of acceptance.

I lead workshops for college professors on how we can help students be seen through relational presence, and they've mentioned that it also helps them feel more confident; it slows them down so they're not just racing through their material but making it "land" so it can be retrieved later. This slowing down also helps them be more relaxed so they're not exhausted after a day of teaching.

Even though students are now on their cell phones or hiding behind their computers, at heart they want to be seen. Feeling seen helps meet students' social and emotional needs and enhances their ability to learn.

> **Invitation**—Let a beloved teacher of yours come to mind. Talk to yourself in the mirror (aloud or silently) about the impact this person had on your life, or take turns with your relational presence partner reflecting on it.

Rewire Your Brain for Self-Compassion

As discussed in the first chapter of this book (see The Phenomenon of Brain Neuroplasticity, page 5) and also in the Appendix, current brain research explains how relational presence practice physically rewires the brain to have a life-changing relationship with audiences. It also nourishes one's life by cultivating self-compassion. Here's how.

The mind has the power to reshape the brain.
—Norman Doidge

Relative to other animals, the human brain is immature at birth and grows four times larger in the first two years. You had 100 billion brain cells when you were born and now you have a trillion. From the beginning of life these cells form new learning connections, or synapses, at the rate of up to three billion a second. In your first month of life your brain was making over ten times as many new connections *in a second* as all the world's internet users now make in a day. Imagine that! Each of your trillion brain cells is many times more sophisticated than the most powerful computer. Each cell connects with hundreds of thousands of others as they share information, forming *neural pathways*.

The learning connections these cells make outside the womb are strongly influenced by the environment. Everything happening around us is reflected in our brain wiring. From our earliest days our brains are hardwiring strategies for survival that determine the reality with which we grow up. The most powerful influence in the environment is the mental state of the primary caregiver, the mother for most of us. And the mode through which we get the primary information is through her gaze.

As noted in chapter 3, if mom is depressed, the infant reads it directly and those three billion learning connections per second go into wiring the brain to believe that's the way the world is, and to strategize how to survive it. If mom is distracted and not fully present, there is no fooling the infant. The technical term for the source of a healthy gaze is "attunement," which is an apt synonym for relational presence.

We cannot fix or get rid of the old wiring, but we are capable of building new neural pathways in fertile parts of our brain that are open to expansion. Indeed, that is exactly what we do when we commit to any psychological, spiritual, or vocational practice. In that regard, when we find ourselves back in a familiar unhappy pattern, it is essential to have self-compassion. The more quickly we remember that it's just an old loop we entered, and that we have not regressed, we can transfer out of it into the new neural pathways we have been building.

Focusing on the newer neural pathways literally restructures and empowers our brain as we shift our attention to a happier life within.

> **Invitation**—Think about a negative pattern in your life you would like to change. You might talk to yourself in the mirror about this (aloud or silently), or take turns exploring it with your relational presence partner, keeping in mind what you have learned about self-compassion and how the brain rewires itself.

Relational Presence in Business

There's nothing more crucial to success in business than bringing a receptive and commanding presence into meetings, whether one-on-one or with groups. Trainers need to motivate their participants; executives need to inspire their people; employees need to influence those they interact

The simple act of paying positive attention to people has a great deal to do with productivity.
—Tom Peters

In dealing with any work challenge, when I pause to find my breath instead of quickly responding, things tend to work out well.

—George Read,
VP of Finance

with. Everyone in the organization must be aware of habitual weaknesses that get in the way of being fully seen, heard, and responded to.

To be fully seen and heard requires paying attention to how you engage with individuals with your eyes *before* a word is spoken. This first impression is the "moment of truth" where snap decisions are often made about your authenticity and worth.

The mistake many make is to place priority on the content of the communication rather than on the human connection through which the content flows. There is often a subtle performance pressure to take command of the moment and not waste time. But the trade-off is that when you bypass the human-to-human element you compromise your influence no matter how brilliant your content.

Does this mean that you need to spend a lot of time you don't have in order to keep things human? No! In a "moment of truth" the best communicators know it takes only a few seconds to stop and breathe, drop any agenda, be still, and remember their positive regard for the other person.

It is the strategies many have developed to "power through" these moments that make it difficult at first to tolerate the natural silences that define the rhythm and tone of effective communication. Practicing relational presence will bring up every bit of performance pressure you may have internalized, but in the end it will lead to an inner strength that reflects your competence.

> **Invitation**—Think of a person whose business you've happily patronized regularly for years; perhaps a store owner, a car mechanic, a hair stylist, a doctor. Talk to yourself in the mirror (aloud or silently) about the qualities this person has that make them a joy to do business with. Or take turns with your relational presence partner reflecting on it.

Relational Presence for the World

I invited a few colleagues to contribute essays on their particular areas of expertise in light of their extensive experience with relational presence. Following are their offerings. I expect you will find much of their advice to be relatable.

Do you know what a foreign accent is? It's a sign of bravery.
—Amy Chua

Applying Relational Presence to Language Learning

By Michael Rost, author of *Teaching and Researching: Listening*

I started teaching English as an Additional Language right out of college, as a Peace Corps volunteer in West Africa. I returned to the States eager to learn more about language acquisition and the role of listening in that process. The exploration of oral communication turned into the central passion in my life and career and led me to pursue an advanced degree in applied linguistics, with an emphasis on the pragmatics of oral communication—that is, the psychological dynamics of human interaction.

In my teacher training courses, we progressively develop a scheme for understanding the stresses learners experience when they interact in a new language. The payoff activity, the one that involves the most vulnerability, is Listening Circles, based on Speaking Circles. As Lee Glickstein describes in his foundational book, *Be Heard Now!*, he developed this communication system initially to help himself overcome stage fright. We have all experienced this in our native language: that often-paralyzing form of self-doubt that many people, even veteran presenters, experience when called on to speak in front of a group.

As with many breakthrough technologies, the foundation of the Speaking Circles system is paradoxical: you, as the speaker, come to connect to the audience through listening to your audience, not coercing them to listen to you. The connection does not come through excessive preparation of content or development of presentation techniques, but through a willingness to listen! Who knew?

When used in a language teaching context, the Listening Circles activity can go well beyond simply helping students become more proficient in listening and speaking. Indeed, it can be transformative; learners can experience using their second language, even with beginning level linguistic proficiency, as an intrinsically valuable experience—helping them discover new strengths and enjoy a sense of expansion. I've witnessed many learners becoming "unstuck" through the experience of feeling accepted and supported in their new language, irrespective of their proficiency level.

Like many of the participants I've met in Speaking Circles, I see the applications of relational presence philosophy beyond the fundamental instruction about public speaking. For me, the extrapolation is clear. Even without the formal structure of a Speaking Circle, I can emulate the model and uphold the ideals of supportive listening, while applying its principles to language instruction and teacher training. While the results are not always instant, the eventual effects can be transformative in helping learners experience a new connection and a renewed sense of purpose in their learning quest.

On Mastering a New Language
By Pam Noda, Speaking Circles facilitator, Tokyo, Japan

I interact daily with Japanese people, who can sometimes feel anxious about communicating with me, a Caucasian with whom they assume there is a language barrier. When I meet them with a warm gaze and easy breaths, trepidation about talking with me melts away. A sense of ease grows between us, and imagined barriers fade into irrelevance.

As a lifelong learner of Japanese as an additional language and in my interactions with Japanese who speak English as an additional language, I recognize anxiety over, for example, choosing the right vocabulary, being grammatically correct, sounding childish, pronunciation, not understanding and/or not being understood. Worries like this can impact perceived fluency at the least and at worst make one tongue-tied.

Relational presence practice allows the speaker of an additional language to let go of their ideas (and what they

If you talk to a man in a language he understands, that goes to his head. If you talk to him in his own language, that goes to his heart.
—Nelson Mandela

fear others' ideas are) about fluency and performance in their additional language. These speakers can now look beyond language to inviting connection independent of words. When stillness, eye gaze, breath, and pause become second nature, it is the speaker's presence that people notice rather than their degree of fluency. The more at ease they are with themselves, the more their words flow, regardless of their level of proficiency in their additional language.

I was asked to make remarks at an event in both English and Japanese. I spoke in English first, then Japanese. An audience member later told me that he felt I had been authentically me in both languages. He said, "I couldn't detect any difference in your presence in either language." He and I both knew that I wasn't as articulate in Japanese as I was in English, but that didn't matter. My essence flowed through unfettered in Japanese. The experience gave me a burst of confidence that continues to sustain me whenever I speak Japanese.

A Grandmother's Relational Presence
By Lois Feldman, psychologist and Speaking Circles facilitator

Becoming a grandmother is wonderful. One moment you're just a mother. The next, you are all-wise and prehistoric.
– Pam Brown

As I relate to my twenty-one-month-old granddaughter, River, everything I've learned in Speaking Circles shows up in my body and in my whole being. When I am with her, I come from stillness. When her eyes come to mine, I am there. She's a natural at relational presence, talking or babbling into my whole being through my eyes. There's a natural invitation from her to hang out, with no agenda and often no content.

Ideas, experiences, feelings flow in the space between us. It is a most natural collaboration. Our connection is alive, meaningful, unforgettable, and so much fun. There is improv, playfulness, depth, creativity, dance, heartfulness. As in Speaking Circles, our interactions can be different lengths with different qualities, different moods, different rhythms, while always flowing from fully being present with one another.

In the salad spinner we pile toy cars and Duplos/Legos of many colors. Then she sits on the spinner and spins them around. We smile at the achievement. We read a book, pausing for special moments as we go. We eat snacks and celebrate the flavors. We wash in the sink and delight in the running water. We walk hand in hand.

There is safety in our developing relationship and we bring with us a generous spirit of kind regard and mindfulness. We listen to each other with our whole selves and with great openness. We notice and take in the subtlest reactions.

I find myself knowing that any moment is a totally new creation and won't be repeated or experienced exactly the same way, and like in a Speaking Circle, I can trust that there will be another turn, full of possibility.

I find myself knowing that any moment is a totally new creation and won't be repeated or experienced exactly the same way.
—Lois Feldman

Relational Presence in Europe
By Koos Wolcken and Jennet Burghard, Speaking Circles International's European training programs co-directors

In 1998 we were introduced to Speaking Circles and were intrigued. We started spreading the essence of the work in Europe in different forms and in different environments.

Relational presence is like oxygen for me: flowing, always fresh, receiving and giving, being at home, connected to all.
—Jennet Burghard, Speaking Circles facilitator, Europe

Some of our participants entered facilitator training and became colleagues. That was an excellent start of what became a peer-led community of facilitators. Together we practice, share, and deepen our experience of applied relational presence. And that led to co-founding the non-profit European Relational Presence Network with the aim to bring relational presence to as many places as possible.

Because of our business backgrounds, we focused on bringing the work into organizations, with the emphasis on a whole team or a company. An important part of our applied approach lies in framing our work in terms of the results of scientific research about what is key to flourishing organizations. And that is that everyone matters. When everyone is being seen and heard and appreciated for who they are and what they contribute, they show up as the best of themselves. In our view relational presence practice is an important foundation on which trust can be built. When we all are present with each other and ourselves, we become at ease with stillness and can speak from a place of not knowing. Our egos can pause and take a break.

In the last twenty-five years we've taught relational presence under many umbrellas: as a leadership program, as the basic coaching tool, as a method of team building, and other applications.

A first entrance is often our Authentic Presenting work. This new way of communicating changes the group dynamics. Participants notice that they become more at ease with speaking up and are more open and willing to listen deeply to each other. The density of old patterns starts to loosen up in an almost "sneaky way."

And very often when people have experienced the benefits of relational presence we are invited to bring in more applied work. Whatever process we bring next to the group, we always invite them to do it in relational presence. Through our programs participants practice relational presence in various contexts: listening, speaking, interviewing, preparing, exploring, brainstorming.

Our aim is for participants to get relational presence into their muscles and apply it to their work and their lives. These days we are so often distracted that we do not notice how much time we "live in our heads" in automatic mode. It takes a conscious choice, over and again, to remember that we can choose to be present with all of our kind attention. To disconnect from our devices into real human connection.

The deep feeling that I'm no longer searching. I have come home in that special place of belonging . . . relational presence
—Koos Wolcken, Speaking Circles facilitator, Europe

PART 3

Relational Presence in the Virtual World

14.

The Zoom Revolution

I've been doing leadership coaching online for nine years and my sessions are intimate and real. Zoom Speaking Circles are a rare place where that kind of intimacy and safety happens in a virtual group. There is no such thing as "Zoom burnout" when participants come without agenda or roles and simply allow the human connection.

—Alex Martynov, leadership coach,
Prague, Czech Republic

Mastering Virtual Presence

Being a good digital citizen means recognizing and understanding the impact that the world wide web has on the virtual population and a commitment to adding valuable content whenever and wherever possible.

—Germany Kent

For much of the Covid lockdown of 2020 to 2022, I looked forward to the return of in-person Speaking Circles, having assumed that the virtual platform was just a diluted stopgap version. But something unexpected happened as we refined the protocol to the extent that Zoom Circles have become their own unique thing. As we develop a personal relationship with the camera lens that utilizes technology to transcend technology, it turns out that practicing *virtual* presence practice significantly improves *in-person* relational presence.

Once you master gazing diffusely through the camera lens so that the speaker sees you looking directly into their eyes, you are serving them as well as you would in person. I term this virtual presence, and all it takes to get there is some practice.

Many leaders and presenters in virtual rooms have not yet appreciated virtual presence as a major factor in making sessions work. Without such recognition, these meetings are often energy draining for everyone. But we have found that "Zoom burnout" does not happen when leaders practice presence and ask it of participants. This will change when a critical mass realize that high-quality virtual presence is key to professional success in the online world, a universe that will continue to expand.

The quality of your virtual presence in your Zoom panel is how the others know you. In how many Zoom panels or other video meetings do you appear each month? How do you show up? Is there light on your face so others can clearly see your eyes? Where are your eyes when you speak and when you listen? A Zoom meeting is also a TV show of sorts. An effective leader with a few vibrant, intelligent panelists makes the screen come alive for any size group of whatever nature. A lively screen is better for learning, better for business, better for the pleasure of communion that relaxes participants into the session.

The structure of leadership in this new virtual world is that those who shine in their online meetings are the ones who ultimately evolve or are promoted to leadership on-screen and off, whether in business, education, among trainers, coaches, healers, entrepreneurs, and so on. Virtual presence requires that you develop a relationship with the camera lens through which you attune heart, mind, and soul with the group.

Format of a Virtual Speaking Circle

Zoom Speaking Circles are one hour long, with up to five participants in Gallery View, so the screen displays two rows of three people, including the facilitator. This is akin to the layout of in-person Circles, where the listeners sit in rows.

After welcoming the participants, I lead a minute or so of breathing to sense down into the stillness we share. We start with a round of one-minute check-ins where the listeners gaze with kind regard into our cameras so that the person whose turn it is can speak into the eyes of an attentive audience when words arise.

The virtual world will open thousands of new opportunities for this new generation

—Anuj Jasani

Next is a six-minute round (with any newcomers going at the end), starting with at least one full breath. There is no pressure to speak at all. When you do, the first thing you say is the name of one of the others, which is a cue for that person to turn to their camera and gaze steadily with kind regard until the person taking the turn calls another name. The suggested stay time with each person is ten to twenty seconds, and if someone stays much longer, I give a gentle signal to move on.

The idea of looking into your Zoom camera when your name is called, and of looking into the eyes of a person on-screen when you know that person is looking into their camera, is commonly experienced by newcomers as counter-intuitive and can lead to awkward moments. But this shifts with practice within a couple of sessions. The culture of these Zoom rooms is to support newcomers and not judge them for missing the mark. Everyone remembers how it was for them when they first attended. Newcomers soon sense this and become comfortable with the format.

Another aspect of the protocol is that participants in their own turns do not refer to another's content or address them personally. This makes it safe to speak one's mind without being the subject of personal comments.

The final turn is a two-minute "completion" round, for closing remarks if words arise, where each participant completes their Circle experience in any way that shows up for them. In this round, you don't need to call out names; rather you can look around as in a conventional Zoom meeting.

Eye Muscle Memory on Zoom

In a virtual Speaking Circle you get to practice, as your highest priority, staying softly and steadily with each person whose name you call to give their eyes into the camera. If you take, say, 10–20 seconds to be with each person you call on, in an hour-long session this amounts to 15–20 times in a six-minute turn that you shift your soft-focus gaze to another person. In two Circles that's 30–40 times you make that shift, often into the eyes of someone you've already been with a few times, and there's some warmth developing in that connection.

Through this systematic repetition in a safe setting, your eye muscles are remembering sustainable soft focus from somewhere in your past, and they are toning up. Eye muscle memory practice can make you into a person who can stay with the eyes of another in the "real world," where public speaking becomes a series of semi-private communions.

It may be useful for you to view two five-minute videos where you'll have a smorgasbord of listening eyes to gaze into. Search for "Listening Eyes Meditation" on YouTube to sample dozens of flavors that human receptivity comes in. This will help you offer your own flavor of welcoming presence to others in a Zoom Circle, or any Zoom meeting you find yourself in, as well as in-person opportunities.

Zoom Circle Alchemy

I wrote here that in Zoom Circles we employ technology to *transcend* technology. Here's how this can be so, and how it is

We look at each other with shy relief. It's the look two odd socks give when they recognize each other in the wild.

—Fiona Wood

responsible for the magical quality and real-world usefulness of these sessions.

In an hour-long session each participant has about ten minutes of uninterrupted attention with warm, attentive listening. This is a golden opportunity to create their own experience. Week by week, I observe regular participants utilizing their precious time more and more effectively to their greatest benefit. Sometimes it is simply to enjoy the pleasure of sharing space and stillness with kind, intelligent souls. Other times it's about speaking what's on their mind that could use an airing.

Or perhaps it's about telling a meaningful story of their life or inquiring within to gain clarity on something of current importance, or in airing insights and ideas they may want to share with audiences out in the world. Or anything else that comes through in the moment, sometimes wordlessly. For those who take full responsibility for creating their experience, these Circles become ever more satisfying and meaningful, and sometimes challenging in a useful way.

What about "real world" benefits? I suggest that the systematic practice of creating your own experience into the listening fine-tunes your capacity to dowse for available listening in everyday life and when speaking to in-person groups. I perceive that, Circle by Circle, the continuity of these turns tells the story of one's life and provides a sense of clarity going forward. This becomes clear when participants view five or ten of their videos consecutively, or a whole year's worth as a year-end ritual.

Vulnerable Leadership on Zoom

At a Zoom Speaking Circle, Alex Martynov, a leadership coach in Prague (whom you met in the introduction to this chapter), did a deep dive that eloquently captures the nature, nuance, and power of relational presence practice, even virtually. In the Circle were participants from Sweden and India. With Alex's permission, here is his share:

Courage starts with showing up and letting ourselves be seen.
—Brené Brown

> [full breath] The thing I'm curious about is connection, especially connecting with such a random group of strangers as we are here, given that we are from different cultures, different countries, different backgrounds. [pause] And I think it's puzzling, and wonderful in a way, that such different people can talk, can listen to each other, and even understand each other. And still, even though there is this channel of communication between us, it seems like there is also disconnection. Maybe it's only my disconnection. I think maybe it's the quality of many people who are not able to connect immediately with others. [pause]
>
> I think it's probably a function of fear of social rules given to us as kids in different cultures. I was born in the Soviet Union, a country that doesn't exist anymore, and I was taught to not be very loud and to behave nicely and don't talk to strangers—that many of us learned as kids—and other such kinds of behavior that create limitations when we are adults. [pause]

I know that for myself it's hard to see people as full human beings, and when I take a walk and I pass someone—it's a human being—and sometimes it's hard to acknowledge that it's a human being because it's a living mystery that just passed me and not an object like a tree or a car. And I'm noticing that I'm becoming too philosophical. I want to bring some lightness into this Zoom room. So, just taking a few breaths and seeing where the lightness is in me. [30-SECOND PAUSE]

I'm looking inside of myself and I'm trying to understand what exactly I'm trying to express right now. Related to connection, one of the things that I try to do as a workaround is to present some kind of façade. It's probably a defense mechanism to talk about something smart sounding… and this is the cover for something more vulnerable inside of me. [PAUSE]

And in this moment I don't know what it is, but I feel that I'm becoming more present as I share that with all of you. I feel that I'm just babbling about some banalities, and I don't like that in myself. I feel that I'm able to acknowledge that babbling is okay sometimes. [PAUSE] *I'm feeling your attention, and I guess as I'm opening up a bit, without the fluff I presented to all of you at the beginning, I notice, perhaps it's only my illusion, that you also become more connected to me.* [PAUSE]

So yeah, I'm talking but I'm experimenting also with connecting with all of you right now, through communication, through language, through honesty, and

I think speaking could be an instrument of honesty, because as I say something I can check in and see if it's true for me or if it's not. [PAUSE] And I'm kind of a walking barometer. I can measure how true I am, how open I am, and if I pay attention to that I can decide whether I'm willing to take a risk and open up a bit more. [PAUSE] Thank you.

Participants Reflect on Zoom Circles

Mike Vogt, New Jersey:

When Covid forced us into Zoom rooms in March 2020, the setting seemed overwhelmingly artificial. It felt so fake and silly to talk into a screen. I thought I'd try it for three or four Circles and be done with it, but now I've been to over a hundred and it's become a valuable tool that will continue to be part of my life. The safety and kindness of the form has broken down a lot of self-imposed barriers that I have in life.

Karen Aurit, Colorado:

Over the past couple of years these circles have given me the opportunity and permission to walk through fear and discover myself without self-consciousness. At first, I didn't quite trust the virtual form, but the energy of openness and encouragement to be myself without interruption or comments has led to greater self-acceptance.

I don't even notice that we're virtual anymore. It's not even a barrier; it just drops into the background. We are just humans connecting.

Whitney Hagan, California:

This has become sacred space for me. I'm grateful that I had the experience of doing in-person Circles where I felt my whole body shaking, and then to come here and have similar nervous reactions that I have been able to work through. And it's such a gift to tune into other humans on a deep level so quickly, which doesn't happen much in the world.

Nedra Hines, Illinois:

I identify as a bona fide introvert, but being heard, gotten, and seen is important to me. Zoom Circles meet that need, and the connections I'm having there on a human level are manifesting in my own life. Putting our phone away and being present with people is necessary for the sustainability of humanity.

Farina Chinoy, India:

Zoom Speaking Circles pierce straight through the time-space continuum into the eternal realm of the heart and soul. They are a container for the best aspects of humanity. They rewire the brain by sending subliminal messages that we are worthy, enough, capable, likeable, etc. It helps us tap into our light and transmit it unapologetically.

Cecil Meyers, California:

After years of getting so much from in-person Circles, I was dubious about trying to replicate the process via Zoom. It turns out that what makes Circles work in person also make them work online: people being open, speaking without fear of judgment, and the pleasure of hearing others speak soulfully.

PART 4

Mirror Workplay

15.

Windows of the Soul

Looking in the mirror I'm drawn first to the sparkle in my eyes—that's the real me looking out! I smile with my reflection like I would with a good friend, and we talk.

—Lynda Marie Roy, life coach

Mirrors are the silent witnesses of truth, they reflect without speaking, they reveal without judging, they teach without preaching.

—Srinivas Mishra

Befriending the One in the Mirror

The primary guideline that makes relational presence practice state-of-the-art for solving public speaking anxiety is to always be with one person at a time. Done well, this practice turns public speaking into a series of conversational one-on-ones. I developed Mirror Workplay as a way to practice relational presence privately with oneself. This has helped many get over being critical of their image. Developing the capacity to be relationally present with yourself in the mirror makes being present with audiences more natural.

But this takes practice. "Stage fright" in the mirror is natural. People regularly use mirrors for appearance and hygiene purposes, but to really look at oneself as a good friend?

Let's do that!

The Mirror as a Portal to One's Lightness of Being

Before you read on, let's first sample a Mirror Workplay session. This is probably the best way to define what it is. The following is a transcript of a session I conducted with Lois Feldman (shared here with her permission), who you'll remember from A Grandmother's Relational Presence in chapter 13. Edited for brevity and clarity, it captures the practical potency of this transformational work. Here we weave breath, gaze, and being *easygoing in the not knowing* into gold. Take a breath and join us.

We did the session on Zoom, Lois at her home, me at my office. I opened the session with a simple directive.

Lee: Lois, just gaze into your eyes in the mirror with kind regard from a neutral place, breathing easy with yourself. See what arises.

[Lois breathes in silence for about 30 seconds.]

Lois: I'm already making discoveries that are amazing and fascinating. I usually don't like to look at myself in the mirror. Years ago I took a workshop on mirror work through Hay House [a publishing company founded by Louise Hay] and I really could not say, "I love you." That was the line you were supposed to use. I haven't done mirror work since, and in fact I was kind of reluctant to do this with you. But now what I'm noticing is, okay, there is this older person here who's looking at me in the mirror and I find myself feeling a softness, a "kind regard" as you put it, for this person. This person has lived over seventy years and her face reflects that. And that's okay; in fact it's admirable.

I used to call my mom "the treasure." I started calling her that when she was in her late seventies. She died when she was eighty-four. I was really into calling her "the treasure" all the time and I realize now that I am becoming a treasure. I'm moving toward becoming one of the old ones who we're glad to have in this world. I'm just blown away by what I'm realizing right at the beginning of this venture.

Lee: For me, Lois, you got right to the point that this work comes down to talking to yourself and coming to terms with yourself in any given minute. So, just soften into the mirror

> *If you were easier on yourself, you wouldn't be so tough on everyone else.*
>
> —Kate McGahan

with a continuing sense of kind regard and notice that you are flowing warmth to yourself.

Lois: I've got such soft, kind eyes; that's what the warmth does. And there's a smile-ish attitude here.

Lee: Yes, and notice that a real smile starts in the corners of the eyes and spreads naturally to the mouth. Your "smile-ish attitude" makes me smile. Can you sense the lightness of being within you? Lightness in both senses, as in the opposite of heaviness and also divine light filling you. What is coming through to share with yourself and with me?

Lois: The most miraculous moment was the very beginning; it was just totally informative! And I'm wondering what's going to happen since I've now seen my realer self. Will I do this more? I'll be finding out. I'll remember how this was. This has the glow of Speaking Circles, the glow of listening to yourself with the kind regard that others automatically provide each other at a Circle. Oh man, not enough kind regard in the house of me . . . for myself. Always for other people but not for myself.

Lee: Gazing in the mirror, see if there's something you want to remember that would be useful going forward.

Lois: More kindness. More kindness, that's the big thing. And remembering how I look, remembering how I really look because I think this is how I really look and haven't seen this in myself in a mirror. I'm remembering I'm lovable, that various people really love me but in some way I don't take that in. I appreciate being loved but I don't take it in.

This is just so helpful. I want this picture of myself to permeate myself. I am chronically not good enough, but the mirror says to me, no, no, I am good enough. I belong to humanity, I belong to this world. I'm, oh you know, like my own kind of tree or my own kind of rock. [Laughs.] I feel like I've really got company, I've got soul company. That's another thing, a sense of belonging. It's like I've got this special, special friend right here in the mirror. For me, this reinforces the idea of essence, because I see the essence of me in the mirror. There's so much essence. Wow! Look at all this essence here.

Lee: Mmmmm. Completing this experience, anything else you want to remind yourself going forward?

Lois: I want to remember how soft my face looks. I want to remember how soft my eyes are, and they are lovely, lovely, lovely eyes. And then the wrinkles on my face, and how the wrinkles add to my face, add to that feeling of the treasure I'm becoming. I've lately been feeling the losses of age . . . eyesight not so good, memory not as good. It's another interesting thing that sometimes I'm just amazing with people, it's some sort of alchemy. It happens a lot in my work as a psychologist. My concentration is so much on the other person so I don't see my face this way.

Another thing that happened in the mirror was I really saw myself in a deep inside way, as opposed to the mirror work at Hay House. What we are doing here is so profound, deep, wide, encompassing all time, having a sense of the infinite universe. One could say this is awesome.

It's so hard to be able to be loving of oneself. This work leads the way to loving and accepting oneself with all the flaws and having compassion for oneself. This is Kristen Neff with her way of mindfulness that has to do with self-compassion.

Words matter. And the words that matter most are the ones you say to yourself.
—David Taylor-Klaus

This is Brené Brown about belonging, that if you can belong to yourself, you're not lonely anymore, you're not suffering in certain ways anymore. But how do you get to belonging to yourself? I think this could be part of the way to self-acceptance. This is an experiential way of getting to self-acceptance, as opposed to the idea of "Oh, you really need to accept yourself and then you'll feel a lot better."

Lee: In working with people who are going through difficult times and don't have a lightness of being about it, I tell them that if the heaviness of life is what they see in the mirror, be there with it and talk about it . . . and talk to it . . . and keep listening. Because when you talk about these things into good listening, even your own, you'll often find that underneath that heaviness is a lightness of being.

Lois: Yes, that's what always happens in Speaking Circles. When people talk about where they truly are, things start to change in a kaleidoscopic way. So, when people are able to talk about the heaviness, the fears, the self-criticism, into the listening of kind regard, things start to change, and some flavor of lightness of being tends to arise.

General Guidelines for Mirror Workplay Exercises

Even a mirror will not show you yourself, if you do not wish to see.
—Roger Zelazny

The exercises that follow present opportunities to talk with yourself, but only if words arise without compromising relational presence with yourself. Even when the exercise includes a topic, feel free to be silent or talk about whatever comes up for you in the moment. Don't speak just to speak, and feel free to reflect silently instead of speaking aloud. Stay with yourself and notice when you retreat to your mind to access content. If you notice yourself doing that, or otherwise averting or hiding behind your eyes, just come back to wordless self-relational presence.

With a handheld mirror about fifteen inches in front of you, start with your eyes closed, taking a few relaxing breaths as you sense your center of gravity dropping toward the center of the earth. Move as best you can to a place of not trying, not even trying to relax or slow your mind. When you're in a place of relatively not trying, gently open your eyes and be present with yourself in the mirror with a soft gaze of kind regard. Your first exercise is to maintain this gaze for at least thirty seconds. It's okay if you start out not liking what you see. That's how it was for me when I started on this path, as you'll read later. Go ahead, I'll wait . . .

If you found that you were severely judging yourself, before continuing to the next exercise do this basic one a few times until you feel some self-compassion for your courage to stay with it. Notice if you are smiling, nodding, winking, or otherwise signaling to assure yourself. Just notice. Does it make you anxious to maintain your gaze? Do you want to look away? Do you wonder if you're doing it right? Does your mind seem to be getting in the way of just being with yourself? Do you judge your face to look too serious or deadpan? Just notice.

Keep your gaze soft and diffuse, not piercing. See if you can get to where you can spend thirty seconds of quality time with yourself without being impatient for the time to end. If you stay with it, this will become a pleasurable, nourishing experience that makes you wonder why you don't do it more often. Some of you will be there right off the bat, no problem. For others it will take a few or several runs at this. In a few pages, you'll read what others have experienced on this path and what they have gotten out of doing the exercises.

Face Your Mirror Anxiety

Even those who've done decades of inner work are often not on great terms with the person they see in the mirror. This is because "mirror anxiety" in our society is subtle and widespread, stemming from the negativity many of us received day-to-day from those closest to us. Those who grew up mirrored by others in a critical light often still see negativity when looking in a mirror.

Many of the warm and wise folks I've introduced to Mirror Workplay had great difficulty communing with their reflection at first. Mirror anxiety can make it hard to see beyond the surface image into one's real, best self.

Perhaps my story is not much different than yours. How I was seen every day as a child by those closest to me shaped my negative self-image. My dad saw me as the problem child and regarded me with contempt. As recounted in the Introduction, he routinely shot daggers at me through his eyes, sometimes accompanied with the words "You rotten kid, ya."

We have to confront ourselves. Do we like what we see in the mirror? And, according to our light, according to our understanding, according to our courage, we will have to say yea or nay— and rise!

—Maya Angelou

Dad set the tone in the family; my older brother delighted in tormenting me at every opportunity, signaling through smirking eyes that he had me under his thumb. My nicey-nice mom would regard me with pity through sad eyes. She knew the price I was paying for being in our family, a price she also paid but could not speak of.

No wonder I couldn't see myself in the mirror through empathetic eyes. I saw myself as they saw me. I entered my teenage years assuming that men had contempt for me and women felt sorry for me.

Over the decades, through therapy and spiritual work, I recovered a modicum of self-esteem to get me through. But it wasn't until I devised and practiced Mirror Workplay that I found a trusted friend in the mirror with whom I can actually communicate. One of the things "we" talk about is the residue of trauma still in my tissues from those early years being mis-seen and unseen. I sometimes find myself in the mirror imitating the way each family member saw me, and I can feel righteous anger and express it. Sometimes I have sorrow to share, but often it's laughter at how clueless they were to be blind to this wonderful young human in their midst.

"You were wrong!" I can say with a smile.

Exercise: Greet Yourself

After your eyes-closed breathing and dropping your energy down to the center of the earth, gently open your eyes, say hello, and let the self-judgments fly if they do. For every problem you perceive, say, "Thank you for sharing," aloud or

Your self-talk is the channel of behavior change.
—Gino Norris

silently. Be as merciless as you feel. Keep doing this and notice if when you say (or think), "Thank you for sharing," a bit of a smile shows up.

The first time you try this, thirty seconds might be enough. Or it might feel like too much. But however long you last, don't ever leave the mirror before you say, and perhaps even mean, "Really, thank you for sharing." See if you can do this at least once a day until you are able to leave the mirror with a sincere endearment. "Thank you for sharing, sweetheart" (or "friend" or "dear one").

Be aware that retreating to your mind is not the problem; as you go on you will begin to notice sooner that you have left yourself and are able to come back more and more quickly. One way of leaving is to be attached to the content, as if making sense and "getting somewhere" is a higher priority than hanging out in the unadulterated connection with self. Just notice when this happens, let go of the content, and come back to yourself.

Notice too that you are moving toward a spacious quality of listening. Even when you are speaking, you are listening. And when you can listen to others from stillness this way they feel truly heard, valued, and connected. Their craving for belonging is being met at a profound level.

Perhaps you'll be drawn to do this regularly. You might get to the point where you can effectively use a five-minute turn of self-listening to get clarity on an issue in life that is up for you, or use it to get crystal clarity before a critical phone call or meeting.

Find Your Friend in the Mirror

There is a famous parable about two dogs who walk into the same room at different times. One comes out wagging his tail and the other comes out growling. A bystander goes into the room to learn how two different reactions could happen and finds the room filled with mirrors. The happy dog found a thousand happy dogs looking back at him while the angry dog saw only angry dogs growling back at him. The moral of the parable is that what you see in the world around you is a reflection of what's going on within you.

I'm not the first to suggest that getting to appreciate yourself in the mirror is a great idea, Self-Love 101. But what's new here is the blossoming synergy of Mirror Workplay and relational presence. I've found a best friend in the mirror, an actual life companion. When I started this engagement, I wasn't thrilled with what I saw: jowls and age spots. Talking to myself felt awkward and it took a few days to hang in and move past the surface, to start to see parts of myself I hadn't engaged with for decades. I'm becoming acquainted with aspects of me that are useful in business, friendship, and love.

Through this work I've become okay with my "resting face," the one people see when I'm not trying to engage or impress. This has allowed me to access a more natural smile that starts in my eyes and lights up my face. If you want to be a more effective communicator, a less anxious speaker, a more soulful companion, start by seeing yourself in the mirror so you feel seen for at least a minute a day.

> *We can still be crazy after all these years. We can still be angry after all these years. We can still be timid or jealous or full of feelings of unworthiness. The point is not to try to throw ourselves away and become something better. It's about befriending who we already are.*
>
> —Pema Chodron

> *It's no good giving my heart and my soul because you already have these. So I've brought you a mirror. Look at yourself and remember me.*
>
> —Rumi

Exercise: See Yourself So You Feel Seen

Think of a good friend you haven't seen in a while. When you've identified who that might be, imagine you are walking down the street and unexpectedly run into that person. Imagine sharing a happy hello and a warm smile. (Got it?) With the mirror in front of you, close your eyes and imagine that scene again. Then open your eyes and give that same hello and smile to yourself.

You might have to try it a few times to get it. When you do, do you notice that even as the smile abates you are seeing yourself so you feel seen? When you can gaze at yourself with kind eyes you can more easily bring them to others (including an audience) in a way that puts them at ease and creates and enhances a connection.

Commune with Yourself

> *Age should not have its face lifted, but it should rather teach the world to admire wrinkles as the etchings of experience and the firm line of character.*
>
> —Clarence Day

I can gaze directly into my own eyes only through the mirror. Of course, I've used a bathroom mirror for shaving and washing and combing and brushing and preening, but to look into my eyes the way I'd gaze at a friend? Not on the menu. Yet eyes are the windows to the soul through which others see us—or look for us. The mirror can show us what others get when they meet our eyes in key personal and business moments. We want them to feel seen and heard in our presence, so wouldn't it be a good idea to gaze and commune with our Self to learn how to do this with others?

My *aha!* around this came with an imperative to find my friend in the mirror; this is what led me to devise Mirror Workplay. For at least a minute a day I've been using a handheld mirror to gaze kindly with myself and breathe deep and easy into my inner stillness. From there I practice seeing beyond surface eye contact, down into my essential humanity.

The new habit has paid dividends. I've discovered how to naturally turn my face into a friendly neighborhood for others to visit. In videos of my Zoom Speaking Circles, I've observed my listening grow luminous, my speaking more magnetic, my facilitation more effective.

Kamila, a designer of learning solutions in Wroclaw, Poland, let me know how powerful this work has been for her:

> *I set aside a couple of minutes to follow the instructions and look kindly in my eyes. I felt this reassurance of my essence, I felt connected with it and this made me feel very emotional and I started to cry because I felt this nourishment and reconnection with something that I probably was seeking outside myself and slowly realizing this is always with me. When I was a child I was actually talking into the mirror to myself until I told some friends about it and they laughed at me. I thought it must be weird so I stopped doing it. As I continue doing this practice I'd like to combine it with a nice ritual, like lighting a candle and setting the intention to spend time with myself in a reunion of the self with the self.*

If you feel as though you don't fit into this world, it's because you are here to create a better one.
—Anonymous

The time will come when, with elation you will greet yourself arriving at your own door, in your own mirror and each will smile at the other's welcome...
—Derek Walcott

Exercise: Establish a Daily Practice

If you don't have a handheld mirror, get one and keep it by your bed. Before sleep, take a full breath to greet yourself kindly without words and tell yourself something sweet or inspiring or pleasant about your day, remembering to see yourself so you feel seen. Never leave the mirror without a sweet goodbye. Greet yourself in the morning and talk about something you are looking forward to that day.

> As long as we think the aim of practice is comfort, pleasure, and calm, we miss the point. The point is to contact yourself as you are, whatever you are.
> —Charlotte Joko Beck

Come from Powerful Tenderness

In a recent Zoom Circle a participant spoke with powerful tenderness about her family witnessing the conscious death of a loving mother. The other participants in that Circle, in their turns, having dropped down into that soulful place, went on to share vulnerable stories from their lives.

The notion of "powerful tenderness" stayed with me the rest of the Circle and the rest of the night—and was still here at the end of the week as I typed this. It struck me that powerful tenderness (aka "loving kindness") is a quality I'd like to flow more to loved ones and to myself. And since doing Mirror Workplay, I've found that just a couple minutes of mirror practice a day has gotten me to where I can flow powerful tenderness through the mirror into my eyes at any moment. Thirty seconds of this gentle self-care can soothe my savage nervous system and fill me with calm for an hour.

> Let tenderness pour from your eyes, the way sun gazes warmly on earth.
> —Hafez

This has become a common experience for Mirror Workplay practitioners, even those who'd done decades of inner work without having gotten past a case of mirror anxiety. You probably already know that rampant judgment around self-image is endemic in our society due to traumatic associations from childhood for so many.

Here are two reactions to this work that showed up in emails.

> *This work is a turning point in my relationship with myself in the mirror. Before then, I looked in the mirror and saw my aging face and checked if my hair needed correction. Now I can look deeply into my eyes and see the ageless, kind soul that I am and meet and greet him in love. Then I might or might not check my hair. This work is an invaluable gift.*
>
> —PK, Boston

> *I never wanted to face myself in the mirror for fear of feeling intense emotions—most likely negative ones like shame, resentment, and sometimes disgust. I am grateful for the courage these exercises provide me. The hands-on mirror exercise began the momentum needed to continue on this path of healing my hidden voice.*
>
> —HG, Calgary

The experience can be one of sheer delight. A psychotherapist in her seventies with judgments about her face had a peak experience in the first five minutes of a Zoom session and exclaimed with a laugh, "Oh, this is how *God* sees my wrinkles!"

Exercise: Commune with Your Goodness

Goodness is uneventful. It does not flash, it glows.
—Ray Stannard Baker

The mirror knows all. It is an alchemical portal. I invite you to commune with your essential goodness by being in silence for about half a minute and then seeing if something comes up to say. It's always okay to start with complaints about yourself, but you'll notice that as you hang in, they pass as you recognize more of who you truly are.

If you are ready to try something new, take a few minutes to talk something through in your life that you'd like clarity on. Without leaving your eyes in the mirror, have an actual conversation with easy silences. In this practice you may notice that useful realizations arise that apply to your life right now. But they may not arise right away. Rather than trying for a breakthrough, just be with yourself in kindness and curiosity and see what comes up.

Laugh at Yourself and with Yourself

I broke a mirror and got seven years bad luck, but my lawyer thinks he can get me five.
—Steven Wright

Some days the mirror will tell half-truths, your eyes clouded by a gray curtain, the heavy darkness of the world dragging down the corners of your mouth. Make faces at it, stick out your tongue, blow it a raspberry till it lightens up and makes you laugh.

—Gus Newport

In 2022 I did a mirror work session with author John Bainbridge, Jr., who gave me permission to tell his story. He was attending Zoom Speaking Circles to prepare for his book tour promoting *Gun Barons: The Weapons That Transformed America and the Men Who Invented Them*. When we started the session, he couldn't get past the "stink-eye" coming back at him through the mirror. He talked about being unable to stop scrutinizing himself. *Aha!*, I thought, *his profession is all about scrutiny, that's what he gets well paid for, and he doesn't have the means to lay it aside while staring at himself.* So I suggested that he exaggerate the glare of judgment, which he did. When he was in full sourpuss, I asked, "Can you laugh at what you are seeing?" He belted out a guffaw and said, "Yes I can, easily." I asked what was funny. He said, "Because it's so wonderfully self-deprecating," which got us laughing together.

I left him with the suggestion that when he sees that face in the mirror he take it to an extreme and allow the relief of laughter. I had no doubt that if he were to do this before he shaved, brushed his teeth, or combed his hair he would forge an easier friendship with his real self that would ease his anxiety about looking shaky at his upcoming book tour talks, which was the concern that impelled him to come to Speaking Circles in the first place.

Two hours after the session, he emailed me: "Success! I glowered myself into submission."

Exercise: Let Go of Your Face

I invite you to revisit the section "Let Go of Your Face" in chapter 11 (page 225) and play with doing that exercise in the mirror. Then see if you can let a smile start in the corners of your eyes and spread to your mouth. See if you can laugh at

Laugh at yourself and at life and nothing can touch you.

—Louise Hay

yourself for your imperfections. Notice that when you do so, you might find yourself laughing *with* yourself.

Connecting with the Ancestors

Two Mirror Workplayers found themselves honoring the ancestral lineage they discovered in their faces. After their mirror experiences, both emailed me about how it had been for them.

Loving who you came from is like looking into the mirror and loving yourself. Your ancestry is your reflection in the mirror.

—Deborah Bravandt

Seeing my face in the mirror this way feels like a portal into connection with the world and with my ancestors. I see my ever-present friend supporting me. In this way of connecting with myself through this little makeup mirror... this little time machin I don't mind the lines in my face the way that I do when I'm transactional with the mirror. There's a life here beyond what I look like or what kind of day I'm having. I have a vast sense of self that is supported by my ancestors who are always there for me. It gives me a broader sense of self that is empowering.

—CJ, San Francisco

When I looked into my eyes in the mirror there was this pivotal moment when I saw my dad, with the squinting lines in his forehead and tension around the eyebrows. I started thinking, "Oh, I look like my dad when he's worrying and I don't want to." Then I thought, "Wait a minute, my dad is represented to me here, so what else is represented?" The answer came through the mirror that what is represented here is unconditional love.

This is when I entered the portal, went through the door. In a flash I saw layers of my dad, then a little bit of my mom. Then there was the aha! moment that here in the mirror is the intersection of now and all of my family line culminating in this moment. So, when I think "I'm not enough"—what am I even talking about? That's not even a thing. That's in the realm where judgment and shame, right and wrong live. This higher realm is bathed in love, non-resistance, openness, meaning, strength, and power. This mirror work practice is so grounding I'm actually connecting to all that is, to source, and to all that was, right here in my mirror.

—LR, Littleton, Colorado

Connecting with our ancestors in the mirror helps us understand where we came from and can open our eyes to our beauty and uniqueness.

Exercise: Mirror Meditation with a Grandparent

Are you ready to try a five-minute mirror meditation with a grandparent? If so, gently join yourself in the mirror and find in your eyes a beloved grandparent, aunt, uncle, or other dear relative. When you do, stay with that person and take five leisurely breaths, in through the nose, out through the mouth. Then breathe in more deeply, letting the air fill your chest and then your abdomen. When you get to the top of the breath,

Breathe in deeply to bring your mind home to your body.
—Thich Nhat Hanh

hold it for about ten seconds, then slowly release it. When you get to the bottom of the breath, hold it there for about fifteen seconds before you breathe back in.

That fifteen seconds of no breathing is where you might find a profound sense of shared stillness with your ancestor. Take another few full breaths in and out and see if you can extend that pause down there for perhaps thirty seconds of communion. Take another full breath or several and see what you might say to your ancestor. Take all the time you need, allowing silences.

Flow Kind Eyes

After two months coming to terms with myself in the mirror, I discovered a key to jumpstart this path of self-compassion: I can flow kindness through my eyes whenever I choose! It struck me then that many kind-at-heart folks do not have a knack for letting that kindness they show others show up in their own eyes where it would do the most good.

> *A moment of self-compassion can change your entire day. A string of such moments can change the course of your life.*
> —Christopher Germer

This led to the *aha!* that the capacity to gently flow kind eyes at any moment is an essential element of success in business, in leadership, in love. I discovered that I could cultivate kind listening eyes by giving them to myself in the mirror for as little as one minute a day.

And you can too! All it takes is some practice and encouragement, and I am here as the encourager.

I remember my Grandma Lena's kind eyes (see the essay Radiate Kind Regard in chapter 8, page 96). She was an oasis of safety for me when she lived with us for several years. My mom too had kind eyes, though hers were compromised by compulsive niceness. I'd say that kindness to others flows from self-kindness, whereas niceness may arise for self-protection.

The men in our home (my older brother, father, and grandfather) did not have kind eyes. I hid the light of my kind eyes under a bushel at an early age because they weren't safe to be seen by these men. It took me so long to rescue my kind eyes and get them back to sparkling in high definition. I keep a mirror handy to micro-dose myself with self-kindness as needed.

After her first Mirror Workplay experience, BB, a social worker in Oklahoma, wrote:

> *I see myself in the mirror often, brushing my hair, putting on make-up. I even do my Zumba class looking at myself in the mirror. But the first time I looked in the mirror for that first minute of mirror work, just me and my eyes, I cried. I feel like I saw myself for the first time—really saw myself. The next day I spent a couple of minutes looking at my face in the mirror. I noticed how blue my eyes were. I noticed the wrinkles. I quickly looked back at my eyes and just kept my eyes on my eyes. The following day I just looked into my eyes in the mirror and a warmth came over me. Some clarity and a little confusion, but I just kept on gazing at my eyes. When it ended, I had this great urge to write; write whatever came up for me. And what came up for me*

is that I need to be me, the good, the bad, and the ugly. I do need to learn to do some things differently, which would be good for me. And I also need to be me. If that means showing my insecurities, asking too many questions, so be it.

Exercise: Radiate Self-Kindness

Think of someone in your life who saw you or who currently sees you like my Grandma Lena saw me. See if you can gaze into the mirror at yourself through that person's eyes. Stay with yourself. See if you can speak to yourself in the tone of that person. See if you can express gratitude to that person though your eyes in the mirror. You might add at least fifteen seconds of communion with this person in your daily Mirror Workplay practice.

Be Impeccable with Your Word

In my Mirror Workplay journey I have cultivated a friendship with the man in the mirror. This connection reached a milestone when I found myself committing to a personal intention for each day. I've checked in daily since then to renew the intention and initiate others. Each self-consult takes about fifteen to thirty seconds; it's just the facts and a smile, a wink, a self-loving gesture, and I know beyond a shadow of a doubt that I will keep my word. In less than a minute a day this new habit of keeping my word has taken hold within, and I sadly realize the ramifications of not having been this honest with myself in the past.

> *Self-care is giving the world the best of you instead of what's left of you.*
> —Katie Reed

> *I would rather be accused of breaking precedents than breaking promises.*
> —John F. Kennedy

In *The Four Agreements: A Practical Guide to Personal Freedom* (1997), don Miguel Ruiz writes that the First Agreement is to "be impeccable with your word," since the word is your power of creation. I know from brain research that as I continue to keep agreements with myself I am building neural pathways that are wiring my brain to be that of a person with potent self-trust. Without such self-trust I'd often been somewhat adrift in life. If you doubt that the habit of being impeccable with your word over time literally changes your brain, review the section The Phenomenon of Brain Neuroplasticity, page 5.

Exercise: Level with Yourself

Take a minute or more eye-to-eye to gently talk to yourself about something you've been putting off that you'd like to do something about. Find one simple action you can take today or tomorrow to start the ball rolling and commit yourself to following through. Keep it up daily with a new simple commitment and see if you can string together 30 days of kept commitments. If you break the streak, forgive yourself and start anew. Do 30 in a row and let me know how your life has changed.

The face is the mirror of the mind, and eyes without speaking confess the secrets of the heart.
—St. Jerome

In Closing

In chapter 9, I wrote about the practice of some speakers to script a rousing, inspirational climax designed to garner a standing ovation (see Your Closing, page 115). But the relational presence approach is to treat your closing as an *opening* to a long-term association with audience members. This calls for heartfelt words of gratitude.

Some of you will find the Appendix filled with annotated articles on the scientific research behind Relational Presence to be useful toward transcending the "tips, tricks, and techniques" mindset in which so many books on public speaking are steeped. Hopefully, you'll remember this one as steeped in the fourth "t"—truth.

This book is a love offering meant to transmit soul-to-soul my life's work in a way that helps make *your* life work. I appreciate your soulful attention. Send your comments and questions to lee@speakingcircles.com, and let me know how I might serve you going forward.

As fellow humans striving to be more mindful and effective communicators, please join me in a luxurious breath of appreciation for the spirit that brings us together in this lifelong learning community.

Thank you!
Lee Glickstein

> *No distance of place or lapse of time can lessen the friendship of those who are thoroughly persuaded of each other's worth.*
>
> —Robert Southey

APPENDIX

Scientific Research Behind Relational Presence

Relational Presence Improves Speaker Ease through Healing Attachment
by Sara Bar-Zeev, science writer

Public speaking involves a speaker seeking to communicate with an audience, and a degree of connection between speaker and audience. The experience of Speaking Circles facilitators and practitioners is that the degree to which a speaker's content will resonate with the listener is dependent on relational presence, or the speaker's ability to pay attention to this connection in the moment. As Speaking Circle facilitator Daniel Kingsley has analogized, this present-focused relationship with the audience acts as a conduit for the meaning words much like a telephone wire transmits sounds. Although our words themselves may reach the audience without this attention to the connection, the meaning behind them won't be fully understood or appreciated.

In the Speaking Circles method, the relationally present speaker seeks to non-verbally invite each member to join them in a sense of belonging. Through eye availability an audience member for perhaps 10–15 seconds (with no need to get around to everyone), where the speaker sees them so they feel seen, the speaker seeks to create a speaker-listener relationship characterized by heightened awareness of their connection. In this relationship the speaker does their best to allow themselves to see and be seen.

For the person up front at a Speaking Circle, the practice of being relationally present without effort or agenda generates receptivity in the audience.[1] The experience of Speaking Circles practitioners is that relational presence drives psychological processes that can support many benefits, including easing public speaking anxieties, allowing speakers to find comfort in natural silence, compelling rapt attention, and developing natural storytelling abilities. I believe that relational presence is vital for our ability to connect with others in many settings—and especially so early in our socialization as infants.

Infants are born with a drive to attach with their caregivers. Recent studies have shown that we learn our mother's scent and voice in the womb[2-6] and even how to mimic the cadence of her native language to better summon her care with our cries.[7] This drive to bond, called attachment, is speculated to have evolved to increase our survival in times of threat.[8]

In an ideal world an infant's attachment drives are rewarded by a responsive parental figure, which cements their affiliative bond. A mother's correct identification of her distressed infant's cries of hunger, for example, leads the infant to associate the positive experience of nourishment with her mother's presence (her milk, her scent, her voice...), which facilitates the infant's reliance upon her mother as a soothing presence.

Attunement can perhaps best be described as the byproduct of these cycles of distress and calming; as a parent improves his or her caretaking ability, the infant increasingly becomes dependent on this parent for support. In this way, an attuned parent provides much more than physical nourishment; the secure attachment fostered by attunement helps the child to develop the ability to trust and fosters self-worth, which ultimately forms a secure base from which the future adult will openly approach and relate to others.[8]

Secure attachment can also promote brain development; premature infants whose mothers have been coached to be more attuned (improving eye contact, responsiveness, touch) have improved brain activity by their 40-week "birthdate" and fewer social and cognitive delays at 18 months.[9-11] Healthy attunement may also reduce the incidence of depression and other psychiatric disorders in adulthood.[12]

A perfectly attuned parent, however, is pure fiction. A parent's own early attachment history can have profound effects upon their ability to attune.[13] Genuine relating with our parents and emotional development were theorized by the renowned pediatrician and psychoanalyst D.W. Winnicott to require an experience of disillusionment with our parents; a parent he termed "the good enough parent."[14] Such a relationship would have some healthy ruptures in attunement (e.g., a parent who is unavailable at our time of need or fails to respond in a way that attenuates our distress).

If we are securely attached to the people that raise us, then we carry around the framework to securely attach to others. However, when caregivers consistently fail to respond or do so unpredictably, or violently, the results can be diminished capacity for intimacy[8,15] and, I hypothesize, impairments in our ability to be relationally present. The main treatment for those so impacted by attachment trauma is a corrective relational experience[16] during which an individual develops secure attachment to another person, often a therapist. I believe that such a corrective experience is also provided, to an extent, by participation in Speaking Circles.

Application to Speaking Circles

A main objective of Speaking Circles is to improve communication by nurturing a natural speaker–listener connection. Initially, public speaking may be a challenge for speakers who are prone to experiencing attachment figures, in this case, the audience, as threatening or not trustworthy. If our family background included an unpredictable parent, we may become preoccupied with our audience's regard for us and oscillate between wanting proof of their admiration and experiencing dismay with any indication to the contrary.

Similarly, we may approach an audience with little expectation of support if we come from a family that was rejecting—as we have adapted this stance defensively. When we approach our audience with an expectation other than unconditional and positive regard—a consequence of secure attachment—we are not fully present to connect and communicate authentically.

Relational presence, in holding the speaker in the present moment, may limit habitual and automatic self-referencing maladaptive mental processes and create a "temporary state of non-judgmental, non-reactive, present centered attention and awareness."[17] Such practices have been shown to promote a state of physical and mental well-being by removing the often negative and inaccurate internal reflections of oneself[18] and modulate self-referencing neural networks, so that direct experiencing of the world is promoted over one's internal narrative.[17]

Present-moment centered practices are also associated with increased parasympathetic tone[19] and thus, lessened "fight or flight" sympathetic nervous system responses and activity. Relational presence may also foster entrainment—a synchronization of brain activity governing cognitive and emotional processes between speaker and listener.[20] The soothing nature of this interaction and involved mirroring may bring the speaker and listener into synchronous cortical activation and autonomic states that promote relaxation, understanding, and a sense of well-being.[21] This state has been proposed to invoke neural circuitry and hormones that promote attachment and reduce stress.[22]

With repeated participation in Speaking Circles and practice in the state of relational presence, reduced speaking anxiety may occur with participants who have developed receptivity to an attuned, empathetic audience. Maurice Taylor, MA, LMFT, a psychotherapist, believes that Speaking

Circles facilitate a type of group healing, and that "the repetitive experience of attempting to get in touch with ourselves, to articulate who we are, what we dream of, and what we can imagine in the field of relational presence generated by that group of 6-10 people who are loving us in the best possible way they can facilitates a belonging experience, which adds to the experience of attachment." A more healthy attachment style fostered by Speaking Circles may be generalized to other public speaking experiences and, due to the naturalistic social experience, may also show benefits in other social domains.

(Maurice Taylor's complete article follows this one.)

Acknowledgments

I wish to thank Julie Hartman, PhD for early discussions related to this topic and Audrey Seymour, Daniel Kingsley, Lynne Velling, and Paul Browning for helpful discussions and feedback on this paper.

References

1. Wikipedia. http://en.wikipedia.org/wiki/Speaking_Circles. Accessed 10/30/14.

2. DeCasper AJ, Fifer WP. Of human bonding: newborns prefer their mothers' voices. Science. 1980;208(4448):1174-1176.

3. Fifer WP, Moon CM. The role of mother's voice in the organization of brain function in the newborn. Acta Paediatr Suppl. 1994;397:86-93.

4. Marlier L, Schaal B, Soussignan R. Orientation responses to biological odours in the human newborn. Initial pattern and postnatal plasticity. C R Acad Sci III. 1997;320(12):999-1005.

5. Moon CM, Fifer WP. Evidence of transnatal auditory learning. J Perinatol. 2000;20(8 Pt 2):S37-44.

6. Schaal B, Marlier L, Soussignan R. Human foetuses learn odours from their pregnant mother's diet. Chem Senses. 2000;25(6):729-737.

7. Mampe B, Friederici AD, Christophe A, Wermke K. Newborns' cry melody is shaped by their native language. Current biology : CB. 2009;19(23):1994-1997.

8. Bowlby J. A secure base: parent-child attachment and healthy human development. London1988.

9. Welch MG, Myers MM, Grieve PG, et al. Electroencephalographic activity of preterm infants is increased by Family Nurture Intervention: a randomized controlled trial in the NICU. Clinical neurophysiology : official journal of the International Federation of Clinical Neurophysiology. 2014;125(4):675-684.

10. Welch MG, Hofer MA, Stark RI, et al. Randomized controlled trial of Family Nurture Intervention in the NICU: assessments of length of stay, feasibility and safety. BMC pediatrics. 2013;13:148.

11. Welch MG, Firestein MR, Hane AA, et al. Family Nurture Intervention in the NICU improves attention,

social-relatedness and neurodevelopment of preterm infants at 18 months in a randomized controlled trial. Journal of Child Psychology and Psychiatry. 2014;In Review.

12. Mikulincer M, Shaver PR. An attachment perspective on psychopathology. World psychiatry: official journal of the World Psychiatric Association. 2012;11(1):11-15.

13. Strathearn L, Fonagy P, Amico J, Montague PR. Adult attachment predicts maternal brain and oxytocin response to infant cues. Neuropsychopharmacology : official publication of the American College of Neuropsychopharmacology. 2009;34(13):2655-2666.

14. Winnicott DW. The child, the family and the outside world. 2nd ed: Perseus Publishing; 1992.

15. Ainsworth MDS, Blehar MC, Waters E, Wall S. Patterns of Attachment: A psychological study of the strange situation. Hillsdale, N.J.: Erlbaum; 1978.

16. Taylor PJ, Rietzschel J, Danquah A, Berry K. The role of attachment style, attachment to therapist, and working alliance in response to psychological therapy. Psychology and psychotherapy. 2014.

17. Vago DR, Silbersweig DA. Self-awareness, self-regulation, and self-transcendence (S-ART): a framework for understanding the neurobiological mechanisms of mindfulness. Frontiers in human neuroscience. 2012;6:296.

18. Vago DR. Mapping modalities of self-awareness in mindfulness practice: a potential mechanism for

clarifying habits of mind. Annals of the New York Academy of Sciences. 2014;1307:28-42.

19. Nesvold A, Fagerland MW, Davanger S, et al. Increased heart rate variability during nondirective meditation. European journal of preventive cardiology. 2012;19(4):773-780.

20. Dikker S, Silbert LJ, Hasson U, Zevin JD. On the Same Wavelength: Predictable Language Enhances Speaker-Listener Brain-to-Brain Synchrony in Posterior Superior Temporal Gyrus. The Journal of neuroscience : the official journal of the Society for Neuroscience. 2014;34(18):6267-6272.

21. Stephens GJ, Silbert LJ, Hasson U. Speaker-listener neural coupling underlies successful communication. Proceedings of the National Academy of Sciences of the United States of America. 2010;107(32):14425-14430.

22. Feldman R. Oxytocin and social affiliation in humans. Hormones and behavior. 2012;61(3):380-391.

Nervous System Resilience and Relational Presence Practice

by Maurice Taylor, psychotherapist, co-author of *The New Couple*

Nervous system resilience—or regulation—is our ability to stay engaged and present, to stay in our bodies and avoid unhealthy "fight, flight, or freeze" when confronted by potentially triggering stimuli in the environment. Nearly everyone has experienced the stress of being teased or laughed at in environments from home to school to playground. Each such incident is an example of negative mirroring that suggests we are wrong, incompetent, or stupid. Very often these incidents are traumatic.

Traumatic experiences generally result in involuntary plunging into unhealthy "fight, flight, or freeze." Needless to say, these traumatic experiences result in a disconnect with our resources—our intelligence, articulateness, and authenticity, as well as our ability to protect ourselves.

Such triggering is common for many standing in front of a group, when consciously or not we revisit memories of shame and humiliation.

My own experience attending Speaking Circles weekly for five years gave me the opportunity to literally create new neural networks associated with safety, comfort, and ease in front of groups. The experience demonstrated for me the cardinal principle of neuroplasticity, that is, the potential for the almost unlimited physical rewiring of our brains. Though past experiences of shame and humiliation are not eradicated, new neural networks associated with success, achievement, and accomplishment in front of a group are wired in.

So the more experiences we have of this safety and ease in front of groups, the greater the likelihood that we will stay present and regulated when faced with challenging social situations in any area of life. The scintillating talks I've witnessed in these sessions by "ordinary" people who courageously show up despite painful social histories are a testament to the principle of neuroplasticity. Every time these corrective experiences happen, whether we are the person up front or we are watching someone else do it, a new neural network for that kind of mastery is strengthened. This is what builds nervous system resilience.

Contemporary Psychology

One of the goals in contemporary psychology is to facilitate the building of resources in our clients that contribute to nervous system resilience. This resilience allows our nervous system to stay "pouncy" in potentially stressful environments, like the animal in the jungle that is ready to appropriately fight, flee, freeze, or otherwise engage.

We humans (despite what we often see in the movies) typically are not running away or fighting. But when we need to be firm or emphatic, when we need to be able to stand up for ourselves in a situation where we are being confronted or aggressed upon—when we have to lean into a situation that might be frightening—we need a nervous system that has this kind of resilience.

Many modern psychotherapeutic modalities include attempts to build the resources that lead to nervous system resilience and regulation.

In summary, one way that nervous system resiliency can be facilitated is by building a catalog of experiences of success and ease. This can be done through experimenting in a safe group by getting up and making no sense at all, or making the most eloquent sense in the world, or singing or crying or being silent while that group continues to hold us in non-judgmental appreciation and acceptance. This experience over time builds access to resources that facilitate nervous system resilience and regulation across all environments.

Ultimately, for all of us, the possession of a supple nervous system that does not easily go into unhealthy fight, flight, or freeze, allows access to and expression of our greatest dreams, our clearest thinking, and our finest deeds.

Transforming Relational Trauma: A Crucible for the Repair and Transformation of Traumatic Mis-Attunement

by Sally Forman, relational psychoanalytic psychotherapist

As well as being a Speaking Circles Facilitator and certified coach I have also been practicing as a relational psychoanalytic psychotherapist since 1997 with children, adolescents, and adults. Relational psychotherapists hold that the primary motivation of the psyche is to be in relationships with others. The therapeutic relationship creates a space where relational dynamics from the past emerge. Here they can be understood, healed, repaired, and transformed, from life-diminishing to life-affirming connections in the present.

One of the core foundations of my training was attachment theory. The father of attachment theory was John Bowlby. He began by recognizing that attachment is a biological imperative. An infant needs to develop an attachment relationship with at least one primary caregiver for their physical, and emotional, survival and development. The infant and primary caregiver attach through a range of attachment behaviors, and gaze is one of these.

A secure attachment with a primary caregiver enables the infant to use that relationship as a secure base from which to explore, and then return to. Infants form attachments with caregivers even if they are mis-attuned to one another, the caregivers do not respond to the baby's cues, or the baby is mistreated. In such cases, known as insecure attachment, they will adapt how they are in order to maintain some form of attachment bond. They may, for example, learn to avert their gaze, be silent, and become invisible as a way of coping.

Other foundations of my training were infant development, trauma, and neuroscience, including the pioneering work of Daniel Stern, Bessel van der Kolk, and Allan Schore.

Drawing from all of the above this article explores the connection between attachment, infant development, trauma, and neuroscience, and the practice of relational presence and Speaking Circles. It invites the reader to explore relational presence and Speaking Circles as a crucible, a relational container, for the healing, repair, and transformation of the traumatic mis-attunement of insecure attachment relationships.

Gaze, Attunement, and Regulation

By the end of the second month of an infant's development there is a dramatic progression of its social and emotional capacities, and brain development. At this time the structure of an infant's eyes is reaching full maturity.

Visual experience from the infant's primary caregiver, usually the mother, becomes the most potent stimulus in the infant's social environment. The infant's intense interest in her face, especially in her eyes, leads the infant to track it in space, and to engage in periods of intense mutual gaze. The infant's gaze, in turn, evokes the mother's gaze, thereby acting as a potent interpersonal channel for the exchange of "reciprocal mutual influences." It is through this exchange that a secure attachment bond develops between the mother and infant.

A mother who is attuned to her own arousal and emotional states will be able to act as a regulator of the infant's arousal. She will be able to do this by attuning to the infant's affect or feeling state. When an infant's emotional state is attuned to "well-enough," the mother matches her infant most of the time, and the infant learns to regulate its own arousal and develop a sense of self-agency in the world.

There will be many moments of mis-attunement, of ruptures in the emotional bond between mother and infant, when for example, arousal moves between different emotional states, such as from distress to joy. In these moments the infant will experience stress. And a mother who is "good-enough," able to attune most of the time, will be able to repair the rupture, bringing the infant back to a state of internal emotional equilibrium.

Re-experiencing positive affect following negative experience may teach a child that negativity can be endured and moved through.

Infant resilience emerges from an interactive context in which the child and parent transition from positive to negative and back to positive affect. Resilience in the face of stress is an ultimate indicator of attachment capacity, and therefore adaptive mental health.

Where an infant's eyes are met with repeated mis-attunements by its mother, and these ruptures are not repaired, the emotional bond itself becomes ruptured. The infant's gaze might be met with hate, shame, humiliation, or despair. Its eyes might not be met at all.

The cumulative impact of such influence means that the infant grows up dysregulated, not being able to regulate their internal emotional states. They learn that negativity cannot be endured or moved through. Their sense of self can be shaky or absent, and forming life-affirming attachments can be challenging.

Mis-attunement and Trauma

Experiences that traumatize an individual overwhelm their normal capacity to cope. Trauma can be sudden, one particular event or experience, or cumulative, experiences that happen repeatedly, over time. It is not the event itself that determines whether something is traumatic to someone, but the individual's experience of the event.

We have long recognized events such as a serious car accident, rape, or natural disaster as potentially traumatic. It can be less common to recognize the impact of cumulative emotional mis-attunement, or other developmental or relational trauma, as traumatic. Yet an individual who experiences relational trauma can be overwhelmed by their experience and adapt who they are in order to cope.

Mis-attunement can lead to mild and severe dysregulation, which can endure over time, as the infant develops into adolescence and adulthood. It impacts an individual's capacity to be resilient, form positive attachments, and develop their sense of self. It may be necessary for them to bury the essence of who they are for their own safety and learn to be or perform a particular way. An individual who has experienced relational trauma will easily be overwhelmed by life's experiences, because their capacity to self-manage and seek affirming support has not been developed to its full potential.

Infants, for whom this has been their experience, grow up believing that such interactions are normal, however ultimately depleting. As neuro-scientist Carla Shatz stated, "Neurons that fire together, wire together." They become wired to these patterns of relating. Future relational experiences are then co-created from this wiring.

That is until different relational experiences gift that individual with the opportunity for emotional and relational transformational change. Change that is also neurological, as new neurons fire and begin to wire together.

And that is the transformative power of relational presence and Speaking Circles.

Relational Presence and Speaking Circles: An Opportunity for Relational Repair and Transformation

The practice of relational presence impacts on many different levels and facilitates healing, repair, and transformation. The Speaking Circles form acts as a crucible, a container, within which transformation can occur. The boundaries of its structure, guidelines and form provide a safe-enough environment from which to explore, heal, and create repair.

As facilitators we are, symbolically, caregivers. We model attunement, and the opportunity for a different relational experience. We come from a stance of acceptance and non-acceptance. We are the accepting, attuned, and acknowledging "'mother," whose gaze meets the participant where they are, and as who they are. We are also the non-accepting "father," championing them to be even more of who they can be.

Relational presence gifts participants with an opportunity to have an attuned experience of gaze. Just as an infant and caregiver practice meeting each other moment by moment, so participants can explore these moments of meeting in a different, relationally nurturing environment.

They have the opportunity to experience rupture and repair through gaze. When they begin to notice they have gone away or averted their gaze they can practice coming back, knowing that they will be met, without shame, and in acceptance. They learn to swim in the warm, receptive pool of reciprocity and mutuality, which is gaze. The wounds of the child that they once were heal through interactive repair. They can now claim more of who they are.

As this is a deeply experiential process, participants feel the repair and transformation "in their bones." The shift is at its core cellular because it is felt in every cell of the body. And that is what makes it transformational. A participant's orientation shifts in a way that nothing is the same from that point on.

The felt experience of their trauma, often contained within their bodies and pre-verbal, can be released. Trapped emotions of the past transform into feelings in the present. Feelings that can now be expressed, acknowledged, witnessed, and honored. The energy of their vital life force is now accessible to them to create from, in the enhancement of their life and relationships.

As participants learn to be with and move through their terror, fear, or anxiety, they learn that their emotional state can be regulated. And as facilitators we are active in the process of creating a new experience of arousal regulation for a participant.

The stance of positive regard, both of the facilitator and the group, further facilitates the process of repair and co-created regulation of emotional states for the participants. And the group, symbolically, becomes a different relational system to, for example, the family, the school, or the workplace. For where it has been a participant's experience to grow up in a whole relational system of repeated mis-attunement, the circle offers an opportunity for systemic relational repair.

A participant, who arrives at a circle with internalized images of how they will be related to, is given the opportunity to reframe these internal objects. They become aware, during the process of the circle, that these representations are not real, and that they are in fact their own projections. This awareness, from the felt experience of the real connection that is present, facilitates the participant to let go of "the story" they have believed for so long, claim what is life-affirming, and thrive.

Many children and adolescents who grow up in environments of traumatic mis-attunement feel as though they are an object, a thing, as opposed to a subjective being, or self.

They may have had to bury the very essence of who they are deep inside. They may have had to create a false self, a false way of being in the world, so as to be accepted. These experiences impact greatly on their sense of esteem and worth. When we shower participants with Essence Appreciations, we are reflecting back who they are, reflecting back the very essence of their humanity, and subjectivity. This is deeply reparative for individuals who have felt traumatized by being objectified.

Speaking Circles provide a relational experience back to wholeness, of self and in connection to others. As a metaphor they remind me of The Ouroboros, an ancient symbol of wholeness, a metaphor for the circular process of integration and assimilation, transformation, and change.

© Copyright January 2012 Sally Forman. All Rights Reserved

Speaker Confidence & Audience Trust: The Oxytocin of Relational Presence
by Audrey Seymour, MA, MCC

The Speaking Circle approach to public speaking is famous for curing stage fright, as well as creating a feeling in the audience of speaker trustworthiness. Founder Lee Glickstein developed the method intuitively back in the 1990s as he worked to overcome the performance anxiety he experienced as an aspiring comic.

Speaking Circles spread by word of mouth around the globe through many personal stories of breakthrough and are based on a simple principle called relational presence. Relational presence is the practice of experiencing connection with one's audience through a neutral gaze of positive regard without agenda, or even a need for words in any given moment. It is the pre-condition for meaningful communication, where a speaker delivers information through the vehicle of this natural connection to their listeners rather than talking "at" an audience that feels separate.

In this article, we summarize several scientific studies that indicate why the relational presence approach causes speakers to gain such confidence and why audiences increase their level of trust in a very short amount of time. The answer is oxytocin, known as the "feel-good" neurohormone that promotes trust and bonding between people and also in other mammals.

Scientific research has shown that the eye gaze component of relational presence promotes the production of oxytocin, and that an increase in oxytocin leads to feelings of trust and connection between the speaker and their listeners in the audience.

Eye Gazing Promotes Oxytocin

The first link in the chain between eye gazing and feelings of trust and connection is the discovery that prolonged eye gazing stimulates the production of oxytocin. Oxytocin is a brain chemical that acts both as a neurotransmitter and as a hormone. As a neurotransmitter it communicates within the brain and as a hormone it signals systems throughout the entire body, all in order to reward certain behavior.

Kerstin Uvnäs Moberg, MD, PhD, a world authority on oxytocin, has concluded through her research that extended eye contact can bring about oxytocin release. Research has even shown that eye gazing triggers an autonomic nervous system response before we consciously recognize what we're looking at.[1]

It appears that our brains have evolved to reinforce bonding with others through eye connection, which promoted survival in our ancestors through our tribal affiliations. When we don't get enough eye contact with others in our community, we feel disconnected and less secure.[2]

Nursing mothers and their infants, new lovers and puppies and their owners are examples of mutual eye gazing that increases oxytocin levels, which we now understand extends to the arena of public speaking. We now appreciate that as Speaking Circle participants learn how to look into the eyes of their audience, they are increasing the flow of oxytocin both for themselves and for their listeners.

Oxytocin Increases Trust and Reduces Fear

Studies have shown that the trust-inducing benefits and positive feelings from oxytocin operate in three distinct and important ways. Oxytocin lowers stress-related responses in the body, promotes social bonding, and improves mental health.[3]

An informative study using oxytocin nasal sprays and a risky investment game was performed by Dr. Michael Kosfeld and others. The researchers found that the participants who inhaled oxytocin spray were more likely to invest their money than the control group who did not receive any externally administered oxytocin. In fact, it was found that those receiving oxytocin demonstrated the "highest level of trust" twice as often as the control group.[4]

Several conclusions were drawn from this particular study. The delivery of oxytocin caused a substantial increase in interpersonal trust. The researchers also demonstrated that the impact of oxytocin on trust was not due to a general willingness to take more risk, but rather it was due to a willingness in particular to accept interpersonal social risks. Their conclusions from this study were consistent with animal research indicating the role of oxytocin in prosocial approach behavior.[4]

Another sign of trust that has been studied is disclosure of emotional events. Dr. Anthony Lane and others performed a fascinating study investigating the relationship between oxytocin and emotional sharing between people of short acquaintance. Some participants received oxytocin while others received a placebo. Participants were then instructed to talk about a painful event from their past with another participant.[5]

The investigators carefully measured the amount of fact-sharing versus emotion-sharing between the two groups. It turned out that while both the oxytocin group and the placebo group tended to share facts, the oxytocin group had significantly more willingness to talk about their emotions around the painful event.

The conclusion from this study was that oxytocin increases the comfort level for sharing emotions, which is a behavior that is known to have both calming and bonding effects.[5]

A third study of increased trust measured the relationship between oxytocin and social perception. Participants viewed photographs of human faces and were asked how trustworthy they felt the people in the photographs were. These photographs purposefully captured neutral facial expressions, so that there was not a bias induced by faces that displayed emotions. In this study conducted by Dr. Angeliki Theodoridou and others, subjects who received intranasal oxytocin found neutral faces more trustworthy than those in the control group who did not receive oxytocin. The researchers concluded that higher levels of oxytocin will "enhance affiliative behavior towards unfamiliar others."[6]

A final intriguing study by Dr. Thomas Baumgartner and others indicates that oxytocin reduces the fear of social betrayal in humans, which would naturally improve speaker confidence. In particular, they studied the neural mechanisms underlying trust and adaptation to a breach of trust. The researchers in this study found that subjects who had received intranasal oxytocin spray did not lose trust in others even after their trust had been betrayed several times, whereas subjects who merely received a placebo spray did lose trust after having it betrayed.[7]

Therefore, as oxytocin levels increase for speakers and listeners through the practice of relational presence, a sense of community and trust increase in the room.

A Significant Positive Feedback Loop

Not only does eye contact increase oxytocin levels, but oxytocin has been found to increase eye contact as well. This causes a positive feedback loop that continues to build trust, connection, and confidence. This fits the anecdotal evidence described by Speaking Circles facilitators and participants as the increased sense of "belonging" or feeling "instant intimacy" with others when practicing relational presence.

Conclusions

Based on the results of the studies cited above, it is expected that regular practice at Speaking Circles in the state of relational presence will result in the benefits delivered by oxytocin stimulation in the brain and body. In particular, Speaking Circles participants can expect to learn how to create an environment of social and emotional trust with an audience, as well as experiencing a decreased stress response. It is our experience through witnessing and collecting anecdotal evidence that these benefits can be felt very quickly in an initial class, and that confidence increases through repetition over time to serve any audience, professional or personal.

References

1. Uvnäs Moberg, Kerstin, MD, PhD, (2003). The Oxytocin Factor: Tapping the Hormone of Calm, Love and Healing. Cambridge, MA: Da Capo Press.

2. http://www.psychologytoday.com/blog/vitamin-eye/200906/eye-candy

3. https://www.sciencedirect.com/science/article/pii/S0306453013002369.

4. Kosfeld M, Heinrichs M, Zak PJ, Fischbacher U, Fehr E (June 2005). "Oxytocin increases trust in humans". Nature 435 (7042): 673–6. doi:10.1038/nature03701. PMID 15931222.

5. Lane A, Luminet O, Rimé B, Gross JJ, de Timary P, Mikolajczak M (2013). "Oxytocin increases willingness to socially share one's emotions". Int J Psychol 48 (4): 676–81. doi:10.1080/00207594.2012.677540. PMID 22554106.

6. Theodoridou A, Rowe AC, Penton-Voak IS, Rogers PJ (June 2009). "Oxytocin and social perception: oxytocin increases perceived facial trustworthiness and attractiveness". Horm Behav 56 (1): 128–32. doi:10.1016/j.yhbeh.2009.03.019. PMID 19344725.

7. Baumgartner T, Heinrichs M, Vonlanthen A, Fischbacher U, Fehr E (May 2008). "Oxytocin shapes the neural circuitry of trust and trust adaptation in humans". Neuron 58 (4): 639–50. doi:10.1016/j.neuron.2008.04.009. PMID 18498743.

Why the "Open Focus" Mindset Works
By Audrey Seymour, MA, MCC

The Speaking Circles approach to public speaking spread by word of mouth around the globe through many personal stories of radical breakthrough, and the purpose of this article is to move beyond anecdotal evidence to identify certain scientific studies that tell us why this work is so powerful and effective.

The studies referenced in this article were undertaken by Dr. Lester Fehmi of the Princeton Biofeedback Center to investigate the benefits of a mental state he calls "Open Focus," which is essentially the same state taught in Speaking Circles. Dr. Fehmi's research was done with the objective of reducing stress-related symptoms, which is highly relevant to speakers with performance anxiety.

Beyond reducing stress, the studies found that the "open focus" mindset also served to increase health, well-being and self-actualization. They concluded that the practice of attention itself is fundamental to the optimization of human behavior, and that a particular form of attention was associated with the production of whole-brain synchrony. This whole-brain harmony is known to produce enhanced states of awareness, integrated functioning, and optimum performance.

The attentional style of "effortless orientation" was shown to produce the best results, in contrast to the typical narrowness and exclusivity of attention that require effort, stress, and tension to maintain. They conclude that it is precisely this tension which appears to inhibit healthy brain balance while performing an activity.

This optimal attentional style or "attentional flexibility" requires allowing one's awareness to broaden to simultaneously include all perceptible events at the present moment. That is, the optimal state allows one's attention to be equally and simultaneously spread out among body sensations, thoughts, emotions, and sounds while performing a task or activity. It also includes a sense of unity rather than separateness.

Application to Speaking Circles

There are several components to the Speaking Circles approach that match up directly with the state Dr. Fehmi describes in his studies. One of the most important aspects of the Speaking Circles approach is the instruction to "simply be with" individual members of the audience, one at a time. Participants are trained to find an effortless no-agenda mindset where they learn to trust their capacity to speak naturally from their own expertise. This is the "effortless orientation" of the "open focus" mindset.

Speaking Circles participants are also taught to hold a "soft gaze" as their eyes meet those of their audience, rather than a sharp focus. They are trained to be openly in presence with the others in the room and to allow the flow of words to come, rather than trying to remember a prepared speech. This is the "attentional flexibility" of the "open focus" approach.

Attentional flexibility training is a process-oriented approach which de-emphasizes sharp focus and the particular content of experience, while Speaking Circles emphasizes the foundation of simply being present without the concern about producing specific content.

The final correlation between Circles and open focus is the experience of unity observed in both approaches to a new style of focus. Speaking Circles participants are directed to feel the connection "underneath the personality" and to move beyond "the feeling of separation" from their audience.

References

Attention to Attention in Applied Neurophysiology and EEG Biofeedback. Publisher, Future Health, Inc. Editor, Joe Kamiya. The author, Dr. Lester G. Fehmi, retains all rights and privileges to this paper and associated materials. 317 Mt. Lucas Rd., Princeton, NJ 08540. 609-924-0782.

Open Focus: The Attentional Foundation of Health and Well-Being. Lester G. Fehmi, PhD; George Fritz, EdD.

Attention and Neurofeedback Synchrony Training: Clinical Results and Their Significance. J.T. McKnight, PhD; L.G. Fehmi, PhD: Journal of Neurotherapy, Vol. 5(1/2) 2001.

Eye Gaze in Speaking Circles: Scientific Research

by Speaking Circles International Relational Presence Research Team

In the specific context of Speaking Circles practice, "eye gaze" refers to a state of being in soft-focused eye contact with one's listeners in a way that is personal enough to be human but relaxed enough to be "beyond the level of individual personality."

Prolonged eye gaze (usually for a few seconds or more), coupled with a breath focus with multiple members of an audience, one person at a time, is one of the primary ways for speakers to access the state of relational presence with their audience, forming the cornerstone of Speaking Circles practice.

More generally in human behavior, eye gaze is critical for processing social signals. We use eye gaze, including focused eye contact and inspection of facial expression, to predict another's intention and mental state.[1] Infants begin to use eye gaze socially at around four months of age. An infant's eye contact with their caregiver may influence the development of typical social gaze behaviors and also directly reflect the infant's attachment and comfort with their mother.[2] The amount of eye contact between a mother and her newborn may also correlate with her sensitivity or capacity for attunement.[3] Shared eye gaze thus underlies and is formative in the development of social communication.

Meeting another's gaze is usually associated with positive regard and interest, although it can be stressful for those with social anxiety, who may fear what they feel is the judgment of intense scrutiny.[4] This may be related to the status hierarchy associated with direct eye contact (e.g., staredowns) in humans and non-human primates.[5]

In Speaking Circles, eye gaze is coached by the facilitator and is an invitation for conscious connection. The facilitator ensures that there is time for uninterrupted speaking, or no speaking at all, and sustained reciprocal gaze. Eye contact in this setting, where speaker and audience become connected, can engage brain pathways (e.g., mirror neurons) that elicit behavioral mimicry, such as mirrored facial expressions and body postures, which is likely to be the foundation of social engagement and responsiveness.[6]

While direct gaze activates brain circuitry that supports processing of visual information, it also activates pathways that generate emotion. In fact, these pathways are often coupled with the perception of the other's emotions through their facial expressions.[1,7] In response to direct eye gaze, individuals with clinical anxiety may have overactivation of brain regions that regulate emotional behavior, particularly fear responses.[8]

Eye gaze and facial recognition of emotions are promoted by oxytocin,[9] a hormone known to encourage bonding and secreted during positive social interactions.[10] During a Speaking Circle, the pleasurable experience of intimacy may increase oxytocin levels and thus activate neural pathways that associate with non-threatening social referencing and reduce the activation of fear. This may be particularly beneficial for those with social anxiety.

Speaking Circles practice helps participants to develop eye gaze and may drive attunement and attachment in their professional and personal relationships outside of Speaking Circles through these adaptive mechanisms.

REFERENCES

1. Graham R, Labar KS. Neurocognitive mechanisms of gaze-expression interactions in face processing and social attention. Neuropsychologia. 2012;50(5):553-566.

2. Ainsworth MDS, Blehar MC, Waters E, Wall S. Patterns of Attachment: A psychological study of the strange situation. Hillsdale, N.J.: Erlbaum; 1978.

3. Lohaus A, Keller H, Voelker S. Relationships between eye contact, maternal sensitivity, and infant crying. International Journal of Behavioral Development. 2001;25(6):542-548.

4. Schulze L, Renneberg B, Lobmaier JS. Gaze perception in social anxiety and social anxiety disorder. Frontiers in human neuroscience. 2013;7:872.

5. Mazur A, Cataldo M. Dominance and deference in conversation. J Social Biol Struct. 1989;12:87-99.

6. Wang Y, Hamilton AF. Why does gaze enhance mimicry? Placing gaze-mimicry effects in relation to other gaze

phenomena. Quarterly journal of experimental psychology. 2014;67(4):747-762.

7. Pitskel NB, Bolling DZ, Hudac CM, et al. Brain mechanisms for processing direct and averted gaze in individuals with autism. Journal of autism and developmental disorders. 2011;41(12):1686-1693.

8. Schneier FR, Pomplun M, Sy M, Hirsch J. Neural response to eye contact and paroxetine treatment in generalized social anxiety disorder. Psychiatry research. 2011;194(3):271-278.

9. Guastella AJ, Mitchell PB, Dadds MR. Oxytocin increases gaze to the eye region of human faces. Biological psychiatry. 2008;63(1):3-5.

10. Gordon I, Zagoory-Sharon O, Schneiderman I, Leckman JF, Weller A, Feldman R. Oxytocin and cortisol in romantically unattached young adults: associations with bonding and psychological distress. Psychophysiology. 2008;45(3):349-352.

© 2015, Speaking Circles International. All rights reserved.

Breathing in Speaking Circles: Scientific Research

by Speaking Circles International Relational Presence Research Team

Breathing in the context of Speaking Circles practice refers to the act of consciously paying attention to one's breath and of deliberately taking full breaths at various points during an act of public speaking, expression, or silent receptivity.

In Speaking Circles, participants are encouraged to begin and end any act of engagement with another, whether verbal or non-verbal, with a full breath. This applies both before and after the audience's applause as well as before and after a Speaking Circles turn. They are also encouraged to take full breaths, in relational presence with one person, at any time when they notice that their emotions are running high, or they find that they have "run out of things to say." Such breaths help the speaker to come back to a sense of being more emotionally centered and also give the audience time to "catch up" and absorb what is being said. In addition, participants' attention to their perception of breathing brings awareness to physical and visceral sensations, which helps to ground them in the present moment with conscious awareness.[1]

A focus on breathing is a core of many meditation practices to build a calm and concentrated mind. Breathing practices can directly modulate the nervous system. For example, research has shown that having a longer outbreath than in-breath tends to activate the parasympathetic nervous system and deactivates the sympathetic (fight or flight) response, helping to calm people down.[2] This may make people feel not only calmer, but more able to engage relationally with their companions or audience.[3] Hand in hand with tranquility and social connection,[1] having a breath focus during mindfulness practices, including that of relational presence in Speaking Circles, increases concentrated attention,[4] helping the speaker to center their attention in the present, relational moment with their audience, one person at a time.

References

1. Vago DR, Silbersweig DA. Self-awareness, self-regulation, and self-transcendence (S-ART): a framework for understanding the neurobiological mechanisms of mindfulness. Frontiers in human neuroscience. 2012;6:296.

2. Lehrer PM, Vaschillo E, Vaschillo B. Resonant frequency biofeedback training to increase cardiac variability: rationale and manual for training. Appl Psychophysiol Biofeedback. 2000;25(3):177-191.

3. Porges SW. Social engagement and attachment: a phylogenetic perspective. Ann N Y Acad Sci. 2003;1008:31-47.

4. Hasenkamp W, Barsalou LW. Effects of meditation experience on functional connectivity of distributed brain networks. Frontiers in human neuroscience. 2012;6:38.

Essence Appreciations in Speaking Circles: Scientific Research
by Speaking Circles International Relational Presence Research Team

Essence appreciations are simple expressions of appreciated essential qualities of a person provided as positive feedback. In Speaking Circles, listeners are encouraged to provide Essence Appreciations at the end of a speaker's turn. Essence appreciations are the voluntary expressions of by some, not necessarily all, the listeners in the audience of one or two words that sincerely express their experience of the speaker and this individual's felt presence. They do not include comment on the content of what was said or physical attributes of the speaker. The speaker repeats these appreciative words, in turn, with no commentary, doing their best to simply "take them in."

For example, a listener might say "luminous presence" or "edgy fun" or "penetrating insight."

In social and performance situations, it is not uncommon to fear being negatively evaluated by others. In an exaggerated state this forms the basis of social phobias and anxiety disorders.[1] Individuals with social anxiety disorders have overactivation of brain regions processing emotion, most notably in the amygdala[2]—a brain region that is necessary for fear-related behaviors and learned fear responses (e.g., phobias and triggered emotional responses in posttraumatic stress disorder). Altered firing of neurons in the amygdala and networks they connect to may result in hypersensitivity to negative words and judgements.[3] Furthermore, people with social hypersensitivity may also have increased reactivity to the absence of positive feedback.[4]

A recent brain imaging study demonstrated that using the word "yes" activates a key region in the prefrontal cortex, a part of the brain essential for punishment and reward associations, whose activity is suppressed by the word "no."[5] This suggests that the words we use specifically stimulate neuronal pathways that inspire or subdue our motivation. Moreover, Andrew Newberg and Mark Robert Waldman, in their book *Words Can Change Your Brain* describe how words can affect action and belief systems.[6] They write:

> *A positive view of yourself will bias you toward seeing the good in others, whereas a negative self-image will incline you toward suspicion and doubt. Over time, the structure of your thalamus will also change in response to your conscious words, thoughts, and feelings, and we believe that the thalamic changes affect the way in which you perceive reality.*

The experience of hearing and restating essence appreciations during a Speaking Circle may thus significantly increase relational presence as practitioners begin to identify with the positive qualities expressed and feel nurtured by their audience. Essence appreciations, therefore, may limit self-referenced negative thought patterns that interfere with remaining present and connected with others.

References

1. Association AP. Diagnostic and Statistical Manual of Mental Disorders. 4th ed. Washington (DC): American Psychiatric Press; 2000.

2. Birbaumer N, Grodd W, Diedrich O, et al. fMRI reveals amygdala activation to human faces in social phobics. Neuroreport. 1998;9(6):1223-1226.

3. Laeger I, Dobel C, Radenz B, et al. Of 'disgrace' and 'pain'—corticolimbic interaction patterns for disorder-relevant and emotional words in social phobia. PLoS One. 2014;9(11):e109949.

4. Cikara M, Girgus JS. Unpacking social hypersensitivity: vulnerability to the absence of positive feedback. Pers Soc Psychol Bull. 2010;36(10):1409-1423.

5. Alia-Klein N, Goldstein RZ, Tomasi D, et al. What is in a word? No versus Yes differentially engage the lateral orbitofrontal cortex. Emotion. 2007;7(3):649-659.

6. Newberg A, Waldman MR. *Words Can Change Your Brain*. New York: Hudson Street Press; 2012.

For Further Reading

Alan Alda, *Never Have Your Dog Stuffed* (Penguin Random House, 2007)

Jill Bolte-Taylor, *Whole Brain Living: The Anatomy of Choice and the Four Characters That Drive Our Life* (Hay House, 2021)

Brené Brown, *Daring Greatly: How the Courage to Be Vulnerable Transforms the Way We Live, Love, Parent, and Lead* (Avery Publishing Group, 2015)

Doreen Downing, *The 7 Secrets to Essential Speaking: Find Your Voice, Change Your Life* (Larkspur Publishing, 2022)

Jane Fonda, *My Life So Far* (Random House, 2006)

Malcolm Gladwell, *Outliers: The Story of Success* (Little, 2008)

Lee Glickstein, *Be Heard Now! End Your Fear of Public Speaking Forever* (Broadway Books, 1998)

Thich Nhat Hanh, *Being Peace* (Parallax Press, 2005)

Rick Hanson, *Hardwiring Happiness: The New Brain Science of Contentment, Calm, and Confidence* (Harmony Books, 2013)

Gay Hendricks, *The Genius Zone: The Breakthrough Process to End Negative Thinking and Live in True Creativity* (St. Martin's Essentials, 2021)

Eugen Herrigel, *Zen in the Art of Archery* (Vigeo Press, 1999)

Scott Hiegel, *Reaching Heaven on Earth: A Soul's Journey Home* (Booklocker, 2021)

Katherine Kennedy, *Speaking to What Matters: My story of learning how to share what's inside* (Katherine Kennedy, 2024)

Gregg Levoy, *Callings: Finding and Following an Authentic Life* (Harmony Books, 1997)

David Lynch, *Catching the Big Fish: Meditation, Consciousness, and Creativity* (TarcherPerigee, 2016)

Gabor Maté, *Scattered Minds: The Origins and Healing of Attention Deficit Disorder* (Vermilion, 2019)

Jacob Needleman, *Time and the Soul* (Doubleday Business, 1997)

Andrew Newberg and Mark Robert Waldman, *Words Can Change Your Brain* (Avery, 2013)

James Nestor, *Breath: The New Science of a Lost Art* (Riverhead Books, 2020)

Nel Noddings, *Caring: A Relational Approach to Ethics and Moral Education* (University of California Press, 2013)

Parker J. Palmer, *A Hidden Wholeness: The Journey Toward an Undivided Life* (Jossey-Bass, 2009)

Michael Rost, *Teaching and Researching Listening: Applied Linguistics in Action* (Routledge, 2016)

Don Miguel Ruiz, *The Four Agreements: A Practical Guide to Personal Freedom* (Amber-Allen, 1997)

Ian Wright, *Dynamics of Stillness: Develop Your Senses and Reconnect with Nature* (Eddison Books, 2020)

Other Resources

John Kinyon and Ike Lasater, *Mediate Your Life Training Manual* (2014)

Michael Meade, *The Soul of Genius*. This is an online video, audio, and written word course.

Enoch Tan, *How to Slow Down Time with Your Mind*. This is a PDF. Tan is the author of *Mind Power Techniques: Break out of the Matrix* (CreateSpace Independent Publishing Platform, 2013). The book is out of print.

Acknowledgments

My heartfelt thanks to my editor, Rick Benzel, for his insight and assistance in organizing my essays into a cohesive manuscript. Thanks to my copyeditor, Julie Simpson, for her wondrous way with words. Kudos to Darcy Hughes, a marketing wizard at getting the word out. Much appreciation to publishing coordinator and layout maven, Susan Shankin, for making this book look and feel like it's as worth reading as it is.

Doreen Downing and I have led over 70 Speaking Circle Facilitator Trainings in four countries since 1995. She came to her first Speaking Circle in 1993 and kept coming back. She trained me how to be a trainer and became Training Director of Speaking Circles International. Together we hold as one the space we stand for, a space I have come to see as the kindness that wants to express itself ever more in one's own unique voice. This book exists because Doreen does.

These are the other lovely humans whose support over the years has made my best work possible: Maurice Taylor, Audrey Seymour, Jack Gescheidt, and Sara Bar-Zeev. Their participation and encouragement along the way have been invaluable.

And special thanks to Lynne Velling, SCI Director of Facilitator Programs & Development, with support from Eric Atwood, Lois Feldman, Pam Noda, Jean Kathryn Carlson, Evangeline Welch, and Jo Anne Smith.

And most of all, thank you, dear reader, for your courage to wade into a book that may well shake up your world.

About the Author

LEE GLICKSTEIN, founder of Speaking Circles International, is an authority on leadership presence and magnetism in public speaking.

Decades of debilitating stage fright led him to develop an innovative approach to solving the widespread fear of being fully oneself in front of groups, through the practice of relational presence.

He has presented his unique programs at annual conventions, regional workshops, and at over thirty local chapters of the National Speakers Association.

He is author of *Be Heard Now! End Your Fear of Public Speaking Forever* (Bantam Doubleday), and *Be Heard Now! How to Speak Naturally and Powerfully in Front of Any Audience* (Sounds True Audiotapes).

He has facilitated thousands of Speaking Circles, seminars, and retreats around the world. Through Speaking Circles International his team has trained over 1,000 Speaking Circles facilitators, who have led groups in eight countries in six languages.

Lee holds a degree in sociology from Brooklyn College and worked as a social worker in New York City for eight years. He moved to California to "follow his bliss" and performed stand-up comedy in San Francisco before becoming an innovator in the field of "humor as healing," serving as Director of the Humor in Medicine Program at the California Pacific Medical Center. In 1996 Lee was awarded the Athena Award for Excellence in Coaching and Mentoring.

Lee lives in the San Francisco Bay Area. His hobby is constructing crossword puzzles for the *New York Times*.

For more information, visit:
SpeakingCirclesInternational.com
Facebook.com/SpeakingCirclesInternational
RelationalPresence.com
RelationalPresence.eu
SpeakingCircles.com

www.ingramcontent.com/pod-product-compliance
Lightning Source LLC
LaVergne TN
LVHW081540070526
838199LV00057B/3724